HERE'S WHAT THEY'VE SAID ABOUT PHILIP CROSBY:

"Philip Crosby is the leading evangelist of quality in the U.S."

—Time

"...[A] quality demigod...Of all the gurus, no one has capitalized more on the swelling interest in quality than Phil Crosby...Crosby's client list reads like a Who's Who of Corporate America, and several of them, including GM, Milliken, and PPG Industries, have won Crosby's own version of the Baldrige, the Quality Fanatics Award."

—Business Week

"An international authority on quality management, Philip B. Crosby is the propounder of the concept of 'zero defects' which eventually replaced the conventional norm of 'acceptable quality levels' in business...among the companies which sought his assistance are IBM, Xerox, General Motors, GE, Motorola, Tennent, and Milliken."

—Business Times of India [New Delhi]

"A prolific writer of books on the subject of quality, Crosby has a perfect understanding of the way chief executive officers work and think. Not only has he taught them, he has been one."

—Central Florida Business

"Quality management is common sense focused on the old adage that an ounce of prevention is worth a pound of cure—except that Philip Crosby's philosophy carries it miles further."

—Pueblo Chieftain

"[Crosby] continues to be a dominant figure in the area of Quality Management."

—Training Today

"Crosby is known worldwide as a grassroots business philosopher who helped launch the quality movement."

—The Secretary

"Challenging and thought-provoking."

—The Milwaukee Journal
[on The Eternally Successful Organization]

"A must for managers."

—The Orlando Sentinel [on Quality Without Tears]

"The executive who spends half a day digesting this book may find it one of the most valuable investments of time he or she has ever made."

—Business Week [on Quality Is Free]

THE ABSOLUTES OF
LEADERSHIP

Philip B. Crosby

Pfeiffer
& COMPANY

Johannesburg • London
San Diego • Sydney • Toronto

Copyright © 1996 by Pfeiffer & Company

Copyright under International, Pan American, and Universal Copyright Conventions. All rights reserved. No part of this book may be reproduced or transmitted in any form or by any means, electronic or mechanical, including photocopying, recording, or by any information storage-and-retrieval system, without written permission from the publisher. Brief passages (not to exceed 1,000 words) may be quoted for reviews.

This publication is designed to provide accurate and authoritative information in regard to the subject matter covered. It is sold with the understanding that the publisher is not engaged in rendering legal, accounting, or other professional service. If legal advice or other expert assistance is required, the services of a competent professional person should be sought. *From a Declaration of Principles jointly adopted by a Committee of the American Bar Association and a Committee of Publishers.*

Editor: Arlette C. Ballew
Production Editor: Dawn Kilgore
Cover Design: Paul Bond
Cover Illustration: Kathy Blavett
Interior Design: Lee Ann Hubbard
Compositor: Judy Whalen

Published by Pfeiffer & Company
8517 Production Avenue
San Diego, CA 92121-2280
United States of America
Editorial Offices: (619) 578-5900; FAX (619) 578-2042
Orders: USA (606) 647-3030; FAX (606) 647-3034

Printed in the United States of America
Printing 1 2 3 4 5 6 7 8 9 10

Library of Congress Cataloging-in-Publication Data
Crosby, Philip B.
    The absolutes of leadership / Philip B. Crosby.
        p.   cm. — (Warren Bennis executive briefing series)
    Includes index.
    ISBN 0-89384-276-1 (hardcover)
    1. Leadership.   I. Title.   II. Series.
HD 57.7.C754   1996
303.3′4—dc20   96-504
                                                        CIP

Dedication

*To my uncle, John W. Schott, and
my late friend, Mollie Mitchell—
two leaders by example.*

Contents

EDITOR'S PREFACE   IX

AUTHOR'S PREFACE   XI

FOREWORD   XIII

INTRODUCTION: WHAT IS LEADERSHIP?   1

Leadership Is Not a System   1
A Definition of Leadership   2
The Absolutes of Leadership   3
The Development of Leaders   4

1. THE LEADERSHIP PERSONALITY   9

Five Styles of Leadership   9
The Leadership-Personality Grid   24

2. ABSOLUTE 1: A CLEAR AGENDA   27

The Personal Agenda   27
The Organizational Agenda   29
Stating the Agenda   31
Creating the Plan   32

3. ABSOLUTE 2: A PERSONAL PHILOSOPHY   35

Creating a Philosophy   35
Learning   35
Innovating   42
Deciding   45

4. ABSOLUTE 3: ENDURING RELATIONSHIPS   49

Relationships Cannot Be Left to Chance   49
The Example of the Bank Merger   50

5. ABSOLUTE 4: WORLDLY   **55**

    An Example of Being Worldly   55

6. THE LEADER AND FINANCE   **61**

    Financial Leadership   61
    Money Is a Tool, Not a Product   63
    Money As Nourishment   64
    Preventing Financial Problems   66
    Making Measurements Understood
      and Used by All   68

7. THE LEADER AND QUALITY   **73**

    Beginning With Quality   73
    The Organization Mirrors the Integrity of
      Leadership   74
    Systems Integrity   75

8. THE LEADER AND CUSTOMERS   **85**

    Customer Management   85
    Identifying the Customer   86
    Determining the Customer's Needs   86
    Nurturing the Customer   89

9. THE LEADER AND SUPPLIERS   **95**

    Dealing With Suppliers   95
    Selection   96
    Communication   98
    Performance   100
    Educating Others   103

10. THE LEADER AND EMPLOYEES   **107**

    Relationships   107
    Selection   108
    Education   110
    Climate   112

11. THE LEADER AND BOSSES   117

Relationships With Bosses   117
Agreement   118
Help   119
Prevention   121

NOTES   125

INDEX   127

Editor's Preface

Phil Crosby has spent much of his professional life spreading the message that doing things right the first time is more cost efficient than trying to fix things afterward. He has been referred to as a guru of the quality movement. In this book, he takes his message to the top of the organization.

I have spent a great many years studying leadership and leaders. Obviously, Phil Crosby has been studying that subject, too. No wonder, it's a fascinating study.

Moreover, he and I seem to be on the same wavelength. Crosby says that a leader must have a clear agenda. I called it a guiding purpose or vision. It is a clear idea of what the leader wants to do. Walter Wriston once told me that he regarded his long-term plan for Citicorp as a dream with a deadline.

I said that a leader needs to exhibit constancy in order to build trust among followers. Crosby calls it being consistent. I said that a leader must have the wisdom to wait with a grand idea or glorious opportunity until the time is right. Crosby says a leader needs to have patience. I think we mean the same thing.

I mentioned picking the right people—hiring only good people who care. Crosby emphasizes the need for this.

I said that leaders must operate at the far edge of the frontier—where the future is being made. Crosby says that they must live in the future. I think we agree that this is one of the things that delineates leadership from management. As Wayne Gretzky says, "It's not where the puck is that counts. It's where the puck *will be*."

I emphasized the need for leaders to think and act globally. Crosby uses the term "worldly" to describe this imperative.

Crosby talks about reading voraciously and studying other leaders in order to learn about leadership. He notes the importance of mentors. He suggests traveling to broaden one's awareness. I say "amen" to all this.

Although Phil Crosby and I have studied leadership in different ways—and perhaps some of the same ones—over the terms of our careers, we have drawn many similar conclusions. Of course, there's more in this book than what I have mentioned here. What I like about Crosby's suggestions is that they are so down to earth, so practical. This book is written for real leaders in organizations, not for theoreticians. For these reasons, I take pleasure in introducing this book into the Executive Briefing Series.

Warren Bennis
Santa Monica, California

Author's Preface

I wondered during my younger days why leadership was considered so difficult to accomplish. Teachers, coaches, and even playmates would attempt to aim a group of people in some direction, and the results were always unpredictable.

When I became captain of a team, I assumed that the other players would naturally follow me. Sometimes they did, but mostly they regarded me as another administrative roadblock in their personal pursuits. The only time I could count on them following was when our opponents had our backs to the wall.

My dad talked about political and business "leaders" who influenced the way we lived. The world was at war at that time, and the newspapers and radio spoke about leadership in terms of military activities. I began to think that I needed a uniform with gold braid to get people to do what I wanted. Later, when I became a member of the military, I learned that rank could get people to do what you wanted but had little to do with leadership. Those who were considered leaders were followed willingly, and they did not always have rank.

When I started working, I found that reading books on the subject of leadership was not productive; few of the things recommended actually worked. Observing those who were considered to be leaders revealed no particular characteristics. Some were rabble-rousers, some were quiet, some demanded specific action, some just made suggestions. But you knew one when you met one.

I examined the lives of great leaders, looking for clues to their ability. The return on this effort was small. The authors knew what the leaders had accomplished but didn't know how or why. The leaders themselves said little about becoming a leader. There seemed to be no formula for getting others to hop onto one's wagon. It turns out that there is none. People do not respond well to prodding, no matter how cleverly it is done.

When I was running a quality department for the Martin Company around 1960, the boss called me in for an impromptu conversation. Things were going well, he noted, and I was regarded as an effective leader by management. Would I be willing to share with the other managers some of the techniques I used? I gazed at him blankly. There were no techniques to share, at least none I could think of. I mumbled something and escaped in order to give the subject some thought. The request was never mentioned again, but it did help me to understand more about the subject of leadership.

I realized that it wasn't what the leader did, it was what the leader was that mattered. Observations over the years have made this insight clearer. A leader may not recognize the personal characteristics that cause people to follow him or her, but the followers respond to those characteristics. That is why I created the "Absolutes of Leadership." Those who already have leadership potential will blossom when they understand and epitomize the absolutes. I hope this books helps many to do that.

I have appreciated the opportunity to work with the Pfeiffer & Company staff on this book. They are very professional and dedicated. My assistant, Debbie Eifert, also did her usual good job in keeping me, and the material, between the rails.

Philip B. Crosby
Winter Park, Florida
philcros@AOL.com

Foreword

There is no doubt about it: U.S. business is undergoing a significant transformation. To navigate these challenging times, we must examine our assumptions and feelings about leadership more rigorously than ever before. If our organizations are to succeed in the years to come, leaders must not only have their heads in the right places, but their hearts as well.

In *The Absolutes of Leadership*, Phil Crosby brings his considerable experience, expertise, and straightforward, no-nonsense style to a highly enlightening and thought-provoking discussion of the principles that underlie effective leadership. Just as Phil's earlier work, *Quality Is Free*, raised the eyebrows (and the consciousness) of more than a few readers, so, too, will his premise here that quality leadership is not only the ability to respond effectively to the situation at hand, but that the finest leaders are primarily guided by certain *absolutes*. For those leaders who base all their actions on the anti-absolutist, anti-theory theory of "it all depends," this may not be welcome. But until we acknowledge that certain universal truths about leadership do exist and commit ourselves to incorporating them into our day-to-day actions, we cannot serve our organizations, our coworkers, or ourselves well.

This book is not about a specific leadership style. Nor should it be. It doesn't provide a series of "recipes" or scripts that we can act out to match a given situation. For this, I am thankful. Instead, this book looks at the practice of leadership as an extension of the leader's *beliefs*—a highly personal "core" competency that can come only from within the leader. While Phil argues that the leader must always keep the big picture in mind—budget and financial issues, product quality, service, customers, peers, bosses, and suppliers—he never loses sight of the fact that quality leadership originates largely from within and from the relationships with others in the organization that the leader takes the time to nurture.

Particularly compelling—especially in light of the reward systems so prevalent in today's organizations—is Phil's discussion of the leader's role in motivating others. We simply have had too many years of attempts to motivate people with bribes and threats. It's time for a change, time we learned the value of *intrinsic* motivation, in which motivation as well as reward comes from doing an interesting job well. Leaders must create the types of organizations and the types of jobs that will inspire people's personal commitment. Mere compliance is too dangerous to base the future on it.

At its essence, leadership touches the heart and soul. It is almost always based on an emotional connection, rather than a rational one. This book illustrates how that connection may be made—only by those leaders focused in their purposes and intense in their beliefs. True leaders know that their success does not depend on their titles, but on the choices they make and the values they hold. Phil Crosby aims to help us make those choices wisely.

Rick Tate, Author, *Leadership and the Customer Revolution*

♦ Leadership is deliberately causing people-driven actions in a planned fashion for the purpose of accomplishing the leader's agenda.

♦ Leaders choose, create, convince, and cause.

WHAT IS LEADERSHIP?

Introduction

Management techniques are obviously essential, but what matters is leadership.... Leading the whole organization needs wisdom and flair and vision and they are another matter; they cannot be reduced to a system and incorporated into a training manual.

Antony Jay

LEADERSHIP IS NOT A SYSTEM

In order to understand my view of leadership, you need to understand that I am not talking about a "system" of leadership that can be learned and then implemented. There are no systems that can be installed to take over the job of managing.

1

Would-be leaders buy books and attend seminars in the hopes of making their plans triumphant. This provides feelings of satisfaction for them. However, in real life leadership is the result of actions taken by an individual. Leaders attract followers for pragmatic reasons; they offer something that the followers feel they need. There is no system that can be imposed on an organization or group of followers that will cause them to accept a leader.

The Absolutes of Leadership are a clear agenda, a personal philosophy, enduring relationships, and worldliness.

People can't do anything well unless they can define it in a way that they and others understand. That is one reason the quality movement has been so ineffective in many areas: it is looked at as a vague form of "goodness." No one can define or manage goodness. We can't be casual about leadership if we are going to take it seriously. Quality is usually set up so that someone else does it in an organization. If it doesn't work out right, the leaders just form another committee. Leadership has to be done by the leader.

A DEFINITION OF LEADERSHIP

My definition of leadership is:

Leadership is deliberately causing people-driven actions in a planned fashion for the purpose of accomplishing the leader's agenda.

"Deliberately" means that we are going this way on purpose with a clear goal in mind. It means that we are selecting people carefully and steering them in our direction.

"People driven" means that we are going to achieve everything through actions taken by people, as opposed to actions taken by machines or nature.

"Planned fashion" means actually laying out a sequence of events that lets people know what is going to happen and what they are supposed to do.

"Leader's agenda" means the specific accomplishments the leader really wants, which may be different from the published goals. The leader may not or may not disclose this agenda to others.

Leaders create environments in which people want to give their maximum efforts.

THE ABSOLUTES OF LEADERSHIP

True leaders have absorbed and understand the Absolutes of Leadership, which are explained in depth in this book:

1. A clear agenda
2. A personal philosophy
3. Enduring relationships
4. Worldliness

Why can some folks lead while others find it beyond their reach? Do leaders know something that others do not? The answer is that leadership is hard work. Many who aspire to the role cannot handle it. Many have the proper attributes but never get around to doing anything about it. Would-be leaders must comprehend, internalize, and implant the Absolutes of Leadership. They must be willing to accept the accountability that goes along with the job, and they must have personal characteristics that fit the task.

Part of choosing leadership as a vocation is the process of acquiring followers by one means or another.

American Red Cross

Clara Barton, founder of the U.S. Red Cross.

The Bettman Archive

Joseph Stalin, Premier of the USSR, 1941-1953

Usually, would-be leaders search for followers who are interested in causing what they consider worthwhile to happen.

The conventional idea is that leaders want to do good. The good may be building a business that will provide jobs, services, and other worthwhile accomplishments; it may be turning a nation toward peace. Clara Barton and Mohandas Gandhi are examples of effective leaders who clearly wanted to do good.

However, not every leader has an agenda aimed at doing good. Leadership often is an abused craft. There have been a lot of successful leaders who have caused terrible things to happen. Those things were their goals when they stood in front of their first audiences or plotted their first plots. Stalin, Hitler, Mao, and Al Capone may not have thought their goals were bad, although the persons who suffered from them felt differently. But they were, by definition, effective leaders.

THE DEVELOPMENT OF LEADERS

In business, as opposed to political and social life, those in charge are appointed rather than selected. Their loyalty then is for the ones who appointed them, not for those whom they are assigned to lead. This means that many of us wind up being directed by someone who is inadequate to the task.

Managers and executives are not necessarily leaders. The real leaders in an organization may not have titles on their doors.

There is always room for leadership, and leadership exists at all levels. Running a store or a family is a leader-ship responsibility.

Many times, those who become effective leaders did not even know that they had what it takes to make that happen. For exam-ple, I have had a good career in leadership, but until I was over thirty years old I had no idea that anyone would follow me. I considered myself in-adequate in this regard until I stumbled into

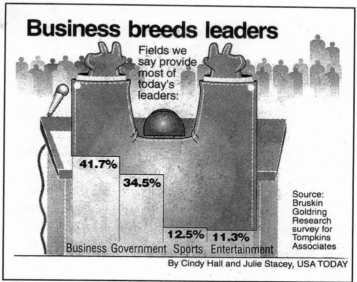

Copyright 1995. USA TODAY. Reprinted with permission.

a leadership vacuum one day and discovered that I could cause things to happen. We need to ask ourselves if we are hiding our leadership potential without know-ing it. The personal signs of leadership ability may be all about us if we just look.

LEADERS CHOOSE, CREATE, CONVINCE, AND CAUSE

We can begin by examining what a leader does and see-ing if you do those things. I list four things: choose, cre-ate, convince, and cause.

Choose. Who is the best person for this job? How are we going to pay for all this? What country shall we invade next?

Create. How can we do this better? How will the participants learn their jobs? What products will we use, and how will they be distributed? How can we explain what we do in a way that everyone can understand?

Convince. What do my followers want to know in order to believe in me? What are the words that lead them to believe? What do they want in return?

Cause. What sequence of events needs to happen? How do we measure progress? What pressures need to be exerted in order to keep moving? What resources do I need to find to get this all done?

The following is a little self-examination concerning leadership talent.

1. Do you "see" what actions should be taken? Is the flow of necessary events in accomplishing an objective usually obvious to you?

Leadership is the very heart and soul of business management.

—Harold Geneen,
CEO, ITT

When you and your friends are planning an evening out, do you suggest that one make the reservations, that another pick up the tickets, that you all meet at a certain place at a certain time, and so forth? When your boss is looking for a way to improve profitability in the system, do you see the flow of effort that is necessary?

2. Do people informally ask you for your opinions? Are they quiet when you say something about a subject? Can you provide a concise comment without a great deal of study?

When I was a Boy Scout, I stood outside a group of leaders and scouts who were discussing the establishment of a basketball tournament. During one pause in the conversation, the scout leader glanced my way, smiled, and asked if I had any suggestions. I shuffled my feet and said that if each troop would appoint a leader and a scout to speak for it, they could get together and set the schedule and everything else without much effort, and then they could pick someone to run the tournament. That is exactly what they did. After that, the scout leader would take me aside occasionally to ask me a question about something that was happening, and he usually did what I recommended, although that didn't register with me at the time.

3. Can you consider the actions and effort involved in changing something? Do you have the patience to see it through?

A person who punches the "close door" button on the elevator at the same time he presses the floor number may find leadership beyond him. Leaders need to have patience, not just because it is a virtue but because others may not visualize or accept things as quickly. A true leader understands that it is necessary to dish out change in digestible portions. Although it is frustrating and difficult to be ahead of your time and feel that everyone else is lagging behind, patience is required if they are ever going to catch on.

FARSIGHTEDNESS AND PATIENCE

Leaders have to think about the future because that is where they live. If they don't have some idea of what is to happen next, they aren't very good leaders. This requires them to keep informed about what is happening in the world and adjust to it. Leaders often fail because they do not recognize the need for change.

Business, more than any other occupation, is a continual dealing with the future; it is a continual calculation, an instinctive exercise in foresight."
—Henry R. Luce, founder of *Time* magazine

During the years in which I was trying to change the way the business world looked at quality, the conventional way of managing quality was deeply embedded in the inevitability of error, the inadequacies of people, and the necessary evils of quality control. Not everyone recognizes the need for change. That is where farsightedness must yield to patience—but without clouding the vision.

The five leadership personalities are:

♦ Destructor

♦ Procrastinator

♦ Caretaker

♦ Preparer

♦ Accomplisher

THE LEADERSHIP PERSONALITY

1

You should never compromise with regard to the type of people you have in leadership roles.... It's not that people are good or bad. It's that they either have the qualities that are suited for the job or not.

Jim Swiggett, CEO, Kollmorgen Corp.

FIVE STYLES OF LEADERSHIP

Leaders come in five versions, with predictable degrees of effectiveness. Their titles are destructor, procrastinator, caretaker, preparer, and accomplisher. To understand all these, we have to identify their personalities and their work patterns. We also can view each one in terms of the Absolutes of Leadership.

THE DESTRUCTOR

The destructor is an insensitive lout. Such people are selected for leadership roles by those who do not have to work under them. They are appointed by the board of directors, are members of the family that owns the organization, or work their way in politically. Usually

Although he has a lot of clout, the destructor is an insensitive lout.

destructors are overbearing, aggressive people who are granted their own way in order to get them out of somebody else's office. Destructors are completely self-centered and see the world only from their own positions. They have no regard for others and find it quite easy to take advantage of those who operate in accordance with the common courtesies of business or personal life.

Not all destructors are stereotypically loud; some are quiet, pleasantly ordinary looking people. It is the actions they take that identifies them.

A typical destructor action in business is to ask a functional manager to put together a plan that brings all similar or related operations together. In a household, a destructor may come to the conclusion that the family needs a larger place to live. In both situations, everyone will scurry about trying to put together a package that will please the destructor. After a great deal of work, the result will be presented only to be met with scorn because what presently exists is considered to be perfectly good.

The destructor either does not realize or does not care about the disruption that has been caused. When people express concern or hurt feelings, they are admonished that only the strong can survive and that they are weaklings or inflexible or do not understand.

If you find yourself in an organization in which there is the slightest chance that you will have to work with such a person, do one of two things right away: 1) see that he or she is tossed out, never to return; or 2) get out yourself, immediately. It is hard to realize just how illogical and changeable this leadership type can be. There is no reason for you to suffer; go somewhere that the destructor is not.

If you find that you have a destructor as a subordinate, get rid of the person. You may be told that the person is "a little rough, but very effective," but that is not accurate. Although destructors usually are very bright and can accomplish useful tasks when they wish, their game is lying back in the weeds long enough to gain control and then destroying whatever is around them, including you. So don't waste time trying to change them or trying to provide new directions for all that energy. Get them away from you or get away from them as quickly as possible and don't leave them any way of reaching out to mess up your career or your life.

It may take some time to identify destructors when you are the boss. They are usually smart and/or cunning. When they are with you, they seem to be thoughtful, effective, and caring. When they are on their own, they plow up people just to have something to do. They have an explanation for everything, and at first the explanation sounds so reasonable, you wonder why you had a concern. My personal experience with these folks is that it takes at least two years to find them out if they are below you in the organization (but only a week if you work for them).

Example: The Coffee Service

A hotel chain had a destructor in its midst. A big part of the chain's business consisted of offering convention and meeting space. The attendees usually stayed at the hotel, had all their gatherings and meals there, and provided continual cash flow. One day, the destructor noticed the number of coffee breaks going on in one hotel. She was told that the marketing department had worked out a deal with a coffee producer so that the coffee was

"Does anyone else think I need sensitivity training?"

provided at cost in return for an identifying sign in each break area. In addition, the coffee supplier provided silver urns to hold the coffee. It was a very profitable arrangement.

The destructor, who was in charge of purchasing, went to a company that was setting up coffee shops around the country and asked if it would like to supply the coffee and equipment to the hotel chain. It had a more recognized name. It agreed to supply the coffee but charged three times more than the previous supplier. It also gave the hotels commercial metal containers to hold the coffee, rather than silver ones.

The result was that the hotel chain lost money on the coffee breaks. The marketing and operating managers were furious, and several of them left the company. The destructor presented all of this to her management as an effort to raise the image of the hotels by serving a brand-name coffee. Morale never recovered, and many low-level managers were punished for reduced profitability in their areas. The destructor moved right along, looking for more things to ruin.

What is often overlooked is that a great deal of energy is being expended to obtain no practical result.

If you think you have destructor tendencies, please hide this book. I wouldn't want anyone to think you learned it here.

THE PROCRASTINATOR

The procrastinator is a nervous reluctant. Procrastinators avoid the world or try to make it stand still. It is difficult to get one of them to come to a conclusion.

There are a lot of ways to sink a ship. Slow leaks take longer but are just as effective as a bomb that blows out the hull right away. The problem with slow leaks is that the crew begins to think it can overcome the draining effect, that it can pump water out faster than it comes in. Sometimes this is an accurate analysis, and the ship does stay afloat. What is often overlooked is that a great deal of energy is expended to obtain no practical result. The pumping takes on a life of its own: people work in well-organized programs; efficiencies are made in the maintenance of the pumps; the center of conversation and thought turns inward; everyone is busy; and there is a feeling of comradeship.

When the United States was exploring the moon, there were a great many successful flights to the moon and back, but the one that received the most attention was Apollo 13. An explosion during flight ruined the entire flight plan and left everyone scrambling to save the crew. The heroism of the crew members and the mission-management team is the stuff of which legends are made.

The three astronauts and their ground colleagues were able to figure out how to enable the spacecraft to fly back to earth on equipment that was never designed for the job. They were congratulated for their accomplishments at the White House. There was no better example of creativity and hard work in a difficult situation than Apollo 13.

But the crew didn't collect any moon rocks or accom- plish the rest of its mission. Somehow that was forgotten.

The Apollo 13 incident was the result of an unforeseen technical malfunction that can happen in developmental programs. In the life of an organization, a similar event can occur when the leader is a procrastinator. This is a person who habitually puts things off or moves away from the agreed-on task.

NASA

The crew of Apollo 13

The pattern is not always noticeable at first. Someone who has reached the rank of leader and has this work pattern may have become so skilled at it that most people do not realize what is happening. Experienced procrastinators develop reasons for inaction that seem so sensible and reasonable that time just slips by.

Example: Locating the Branch Office

Jim Fergueson entered the CEO's office, report in hand, smile on face, ready to complete his assignment. The CEO, in shirtsleeves, was standing in front of the planning chart that covered the side wall of the office. He greeted Jim and turned back to the chart. The CEO had been in this job for only six months, but during that time he had succeeded in getting the senior staff members to work together in planning the organization's future. Everyone liked him.

"Well Jim," he said, "have you found the place to put our new branch office? I have a pin here in my hand to stick right in the map when you tell me."

Jim smiled. "Yes, sir," he replied. "We surveyed eight cities as you suggested. I have the results here in this report."

"Let's cut to the chase," said the CEO. "We need to get this set up quickly. Where is it going to be? I wanted those who are going to be responsible for making it work to select the location."

"It comes down to Wheeling, West Virginia. It has a great location, right in the center of the Eastern half of the nation; it has good transportation; it is near Pittsburgh; the housing prices are low; there are several colleges in Wheeling itself and nearby; and the labor pool is inexpensive. Oh, it also has health-care facilities that are quite sophisticated. We have identified a building that will give us a temporary lease arrangement, and the city will cooperate in helping us build our own warehouse and office."

Jim continued, "If you are interested, Mayor Baller has offered to come over and talk with you about it."

The CEO smiled and nodded. "Sounds as though you have made a good and careful choice. I have been to Wheeling, and it is an nice place. They have a great park there, Oglebay, which might mean that you would get a lot of headquarter visitors."

"So, we can go ahead, sir?," asked Jim. "I'm prepared to sign the lease today and have the office up and running in three weeks."

"Sounds good to me, Jim," said the CEO. "I would like to take a look at the lease before the actual signing, and it would be nice to have a chat with the mayor. When do you think he could come over here? I wouldn't want to inconvenience him; we could send a plane if that would help. And after that, I want to tell the board members about it—some of them were interested in where we would put this branch. The next meeting is in three weeks. Perhaps you would like to come make a presentation on your selection?"

"I didn't realize that the board had to approve this transaction," said Jim.

The CEO walked over, placed his hand on Jim's shoulder, and re-marked that it was always a good idea to keep the board informed. "Besides," he said, "it will give me a chance to show you off."

Flattered, Jim agreed, leaving the office to begin his preparation for the board meeting. He sent the lease to the CEO's office the next day, after the legal department had blessed the wording and accounting had reserved the funds. He worked with the human resources group to identify the core group of people who would be transferred to Wheeling in order to set up the office. When the day of the board meeting arrived, Jim had prepared photographs, charts, an organization plan, a video of Wheeling officials welcoming the company, and a five-minute, concise speech on just what the new branch office would accomplish for the company.

Several years ago, *Fortune* identified the term "empty suit" to describe a manager who doesn't want to make a mistake or doesn't want to offend anyone, so never makes a decision.[1] The CEO in this example is such a person: much form, little substance; much activity, little accomplishment. The empty suit who rises quickly in the ranks has moved on before the results of his or her inactivity are apparent. According to Allan Cohen, a management professor at Boston College: "The higher you go, the longer it takes anybody to tell whether or not you're doing a good job."

At the appointed time, Jim sat in the hall adjacent to the board-meeting room. His material was already mounted inside, so he was left with nothing to do except try to look like this was a normal day's work for him. Around noon, the board's secretary came out to tell him that the outside directors had not quite finished their committee sessions, so the agenda was behind schedule. He could go to lunch and be back in an hour. Jim agreed and went out to find something to eat. However, he wound up walking around, trying to relax and look like a budding executive. He had made himself promise not to change any of his planned presentation. He never did eat anything.

At four thirty, the CEO came out to hall to tell Jim that the board had gotten so involved in a couple of financial problems that it would not be able to include him in the remaining agenda. He would be scheduled for the early part of the next meeting, in one month. He was sorry.

Before Jim could ask about the status of the branch office, the CEO had returned to the meeting.

During the next few weeks, Jim attempted to get an answer about the office, to no avail. He was fielding calls from human resources, Wheeling officials, department heads who would be having operations there, and people who wanted jobs in Wheeling. When the board meeting finally came, Jim was asked to provide a paper that the directors could read rather than make a presentation. He put this together quickly, and the board's secretary got it out to everyone.

After a few days, Jim asked if there were any questions or problems and was told that everyone seemed to like his report and there were no problems. A hurried hallway chat with the CEO revealed that he was anxious to get on with the venture but felt that since several months had elapsed, Jim should make a quick review to make sure all the information was still correct. Jim pointed out that this would require a few weeks, as all the people involved in the original survey had returned to their departments. The CEO said that he didn't want anything special, just some reassurance that Jim was still certain that Wheeling was the place.

At home that night, Jim received a call from an executive-search firm. He learned from the caller that he had been identified as just the type of person an unidentified company was looking for to direct an operation that would set up and run its branch offices around the U.S. He would not have to do much traveling on a regular basis. The company wanted to establish an office in each of the top twenty-one regions of the U.S. It didn't want to be in big cities, but wanted to be able to deliver to them easily with its truck network.

"Who gets to decide where the branch office goes, and who has the final word?" Jim asked.

"You would, of course," said the interviewer. "This company wants to move fast."

After meeting with his prospective boss and learning about the company's management policies, Jim returned to his company and handed in his resignation. The CEO asked to talk with him before he left, and Jim went over to his office, waiting for an

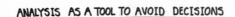

ANALYSIS AS A TOOL TO AVOID DECISIONS

THE PURPOSE OF ANALYSIS IS TO AVOID MAKING HARD DECISIONS. THEREFORE, THERE CAN NEVER BE TOO MUCH ANALYSIS.

DID YOU DO A PRESENT VALUE ANALYSIS?

YES.

ENVIRONMENTAL STUDY?
YES
BUDGET ANALYSIS?
YES
STOCKHOLDER IMPACT?
YES
CARBON DATING?
UH...NO

WELL, THEN YOU'RE WASTING MY TIME, AREN'T YOU.

DILBERT reprinted by permission of United Feature Syndicate, Inc.

Psychologist Harry Levinson notes, "People who handle things expediently are often people who can't sense what's going on beneath them." Information stops flowing upward. The best people, tired of looking to their empty-suit bosses for direction that never comes, soon go elsewhere.[2]

hour until he could be seen. The CEO said that he was concerned that Jim wanted to leave because there was a good future for him in the present company. He asked whether Jim had a reason except for money and perks.

Jim stalled a little but finally said that he felt it was difficult to get things done in the present company. He had been working for six months on the Wheeling office, and it still was not approved.

"Well, it would have been all wrapped up within a few more weeks," said the CEO, "but now we'll have to start over, with you leaving."

They parted with smiles and handshakes.

In his new job, Jim put a new office in Wheeling. His old company never set one up anywhere. The CEO taught his company to work hard at not getting things finished. It always seemed as if something were going to happen, and there always was something going on, but results were rare. Everyone was busy pumping water instead of eliminating the leaks.

The procrastinator leader is a kinder, gentler person than the destructor, but the effect is basically the same. What the destructor does on purpose, the procrastinator does by inaction. But dead is dead, no matter how you get there.

THE CARETAKER

The caretaker is frozen in time. Caretakers determine the best year they ever had and spend their time trying to live it over again. When you talk with them they tell you how it is necessary for you to understand the way the business works.

Example: The Political Party

A political party had been in office for many years in a Midwestern state. With successful elections just over, the leaders gathered for a strategy session. Party chairman

Wendell Andersen greeted each attendee by name. As members assembled in the conference area, Andersen worked his way to the front of the room and called the meeting to order. He congratulated the group on the hard work that made the successful election possible and identified several individuals. The governor arrived and was welcomed by all. Then the chairman began to speak.

"We have had a great campaign. Now there is the job of governing, which is up to those of you who now hold office. The party's job is to stay healthy and get ready for the next election. That means organization, and that means communicating with the members around the state. We already have a good telephone and fax system, offices in the major cities, and a schedule for fund-raising meetings."

"We are not going to be caught with our pants down; we are going to be ready for whatever happens. This party has been winning elections in this state for two generations and it will win the next one. All we have to do is what has worked in the past."

Sharon Michaels raised her hand. "I think, Mr. Chairman, that the new generation is going to require something more than what has happened in the past."

The chairman smiled. "We certainly are always open to new ideas, Sharon. What sort of things do you have in mind?"

"Well, there are two or three I have been thinking about. One is that there are a lot of new ways of communicating now,

All those opposed, signify by saying, "I quit."

George Crenshaw

like electronic mail. You can leave messages for people that they can't ignore. Another is that we might need to set up a school to teach people how to be good public servants. It could also teach them how to campaign. Many of our winning margins were much smaller this time than before."

The chairman nodded. "Yes, that is true; some of the margins were smaller. That is why we need to get started earlier this time, doing what we know how to do. I don't have e-mail and I think it is a passing fancy. But we can check it out. Anyone else have anything they would like to bring up?"

"Our party membership is getting older," said Val Rymer. "I noticed that at the Governor's inauguration. There were a lot more gray heads."

"I think a lot of that was because of how much you charged people to come to the inauguration," the Governor responded. "I think the next time it needs to be more open."

The chairman shook his head. "It is a great place to raise money, the people are honored to come, and it binds them us by being somewhat exclusive."

Sharon stood up. "But that is just the problem; a lot of people feel left out. They don't feel any relationship to our party. I think we have to take a different view. 'Exclusive' isn't going to win over the voters anymore."

The chairman became irritated. "Look, when you have been in politics as long as I have, you will understand that there is only one way to build a party, finance it, and win elections. If we start having a college for candidates, and communicating with computers, and shutting out our older members, we'll be out on the street. I'm willing to talk about anything but it needs to be thought out first. As long as I am chairman, that is the way we will do things."

The example shows a caretaker focusing on what worked in the past and trying to make it more effective

I**n 1956, IBM executives said they were not interested in building computers because there would be a market for only about ten big ones.**[3]

while ignoring what is going on in the present or what will be needed in the future. Many well-known corporations, including General Motors, Xerox, Kodak, Sears, Chrysler, Ford, and IBM, have published reports of how they recovered their markets after suffering losses due to competitive pressures. After World War II, several steel companies in the U.S. spent huge sums rebuilding their plants, but they duplicated what they had done before rather than moving into new technology. All these corporations became so convinced of their own correctness that they locked into doing the same things year after year. That is what the caretaker leader does: plants the same crop until the field is worn out.

Even individuals need to change in order to progress. I wrote my first book on an upright Underwood typewriter. It had metal keys, a ribbon, a black roller that moved the paper forward, and an extended arm that was used to start a new line. When I made an error, it was necessary to erase the mark from the paper and begin again. If I wanted a duplicate copy, I had to place carbon paper between the sheets, which meant several pages had to be erased if I got something wrong.

When electric typewriters came in, I got a thirty-pound, "portable" SCM machine that did the same things as the mechanical one with a lot less effort. Everything was the same, including erasing errors, but pressing the keys and causing the carriage to return were easier. I kept looking for some way to avoid the painful physical work of writing. The next step was a twenty-one pound machine that actually could be carried around. Although it was still mechanical, it enabled me to write while I was traveling. I wrote all my books at home, on airplanes, and in hotel rooms, when I had uninterrupted time.

Now computers are common, and the advantages are obvious. I can write a whole book and transmit it to the publisher without ever seeing a piece of paper. I used to have to have it all typed out, reprinted and put

IBM initially forecast a total market for 200,000 personal computers. By the end of 1992, almost twice that number sold each week.[4]

© 1994 FPG Intl

Underwood Typewriter

© Dennis O'Clair/Tony Stone Images

Modern PC

into six three-ring binders, lug the whole batch on an airplane, and give it to my publisher, who would lug it all back to his office. I now send a book in by modem and carry a disk in my pocket to the publisher. My family communicates with me by electronic mail, and all my materials are on disk.

One adapts, learns, makes changes, and progresses if one is concerned with meeting goals in new (better) way. The political party in the example needs more than money and telephones; it needs to know exactly what the electorate wants from its leaders and how to present itself properly to them. Voters are better educated and much more informed that they used to be; they have television news and print media to inform them, and—like other customers—they cannot be taken for granted. They change continually in every respect.

Caretakers, like destructors and procrastinators, do not recognize talent when they see it. They tend to select those who are predictable while setting aside those who have true value. It takes a person who is confident in his or her own abilities and intelligence to champion those with the potential for leadership.

THE PREPARER

The preparer focuses on planned progress. The preparer leadership style is about dealing with the real world, in real time. Preparers are interested in what they can learn from you. They want to add to their knowledge. They want to know what is out there. They ask questions, they are easy to be with, and they are helpful. They are the Lewis and Clark of the organizational world. They have no problems in tossing aside what worked in the past when they see that the future needs something different. But they have firm principles that are timeless: be prepared; stay close to the customers; don't make trouble for yourself; and decide what to do and then have that done right the first time, every time.

Example: The 1994 Election

In the U.S. elections of 1994, the Republican party knew that the voters were upset with the Congress, viewing it as a tax-and-spend organization. Overall, Congressional members were seen as interested only in being reelected and caring nothing for the future, although many voters were still loyal to their particular members of Congress. The Republicans surveyed the populace about its concerns, took the top ten concerns (crime, the deficit, and such), and established the "Contract with America." "Elect us and we will do something about these ten concerns and do it in one-hundred days," they said. "But we need a majority in both houses. Put your country first."

For the first time in U.S. history, voters had the sense of voting for the whole Congress. The Republican party was able to separate the individual members of Congress from the loyalty of their districts. Even the Speaker of the House failed to be reelected. The Republicans recognized that people seriously wanted change, so they made a deliberate change in the way they ran their campaign strategy. It worked.

THE ACCOMPLISHER

The accomplisher is vibrantly consistent. This leader has it all together: relationships are successful, transactions are complete, strategies are well thought out and communicated, people are proud to be working with the accomplisher, and most business and personal interactions are successful. You recognize an accomplisher when you come across one.

The best way to explain an accomplisher is to present the Absolutes of Leadership. The following chapters deal with these in depth. Taken together, they draw a profile of the accomplisher leader.

THE LEADERSHIP-PERSONALITY GRID

The Leadership-Personality Grid helps to identify the various types of leaders. This grid lets you examine those types you have been assigned to follow. It also lets you take a look at the way you operate in a leadership role. You may or may not be pleased with what you discover, but most leadership practices can benefit from improvement.

Leadership-Personality Grid

	Destructor	Procrastinator	Caretaker	Preparer	Accomplisher
Agenda	"We'll do it this way now."	"I'll get back to you later on this."	"Make sure this doesn't violate any laws."	"Lay out the strategy so eveyone can see it."	"We will review milestones each month."
Philosophy	"I know more than you do."	"Let's not rush things."	"If it isn't broken, don't fix it."	"I want us to be consistent in all things."	"I want everyone to know our philosophy."
Relationships	"I don't need anyone."	"Let's see how they work out first."	"We'll do what worked the last time."	"We need to have more seminars."	"Include customers, suppliers, and employees."
What We See:	Insensitive Lout	Nervously Reluctant	Frozen in Time	Planned Progress	Vibrantly Consistent

REFLECTIONS

The five types of leaders can be identified by their personalities and their work patterns.

- ◆ Regardless of how amenable they may seem initially, destructors see things only from their own points of view and have no regard for others. A destructor does not care if he or she wreaks havoc with the schedules, work lives, and careers of others.

- ◆ Procrastinators waste a lot of other people's time and energy. Data gathering and studying may go on endlessly as the procrastinator avoids coming to a conclusion, making a decision, or ending a project.

- ◆ The caretaker wants things to stay the way they were, to "know the ropes," avoid change, and establish a feeling of security and solidity. The caretaker may fear the unknown, fear his or her ability to keep up or adapt, or have turf to protect.

- ◆ The preparer is a planner. Although the preparer is interested in learning, exploring the possibilities and laying the trail may be more interesting to him or her than following through. Preparers tend not to be flexible in the face of rapid change.

- ◆ The accomplisher exemplifies the Absolutes of Leadership. The characteristics of the accomplisher are described in the following chapters of this book.

♦ A successful leader has two agendas: one personal, the other organizational.

♦ The purpose of an organizational agenda is to establish the framework within which all work is done.

ABSOLUTE 1:
A CLEAR AGENDA

The source of good management is found in the imagination of leaders, persons who form new visions and manifest them with a high degree of craft. The blending of vision and craft communicates the purpose.

Henry M. Boettinger,
Director of Corporate Planning, AT&T

2

THE PERSONAL AGENDA

The accomplisher, as a successful leader, has two agendas: one personal, the other organizational. The personal agenda concerns the goals close to the leader's heart and the process of attaining them. It relates to what the individual wants for himself or herself. Accomplishers recognize that organizations are vehicles, platforms on which they can mount the events that need to occur. A particular effort may be just a step along a well-thought-out path or it may be the end of the road.

The accomplisher deals in long-range goals and considers personal

In dreams begins responsibility.
—William Butler Yeats

questions in defining them. These questions are different for each person, but some are:

- "What do I want to accomplish by age forty? Forty-five? Fifty?"
- "What do I want my financial status to be?"
- How do my family members figure in this? What is the best way to care for them without putting burdens in their way?"
- "What type of recognition do I want?"
- "How will I know when each phase of my plan is complete?"

For most leaders, the long-range personal goal can be stated in a few words: become President, win the Nobel prize, join the Forbes 400, be recognized as the ultimate organizer, clean up the oceans; save the whales; establish the new religion, set up a successful chain of grocery stores, be father of the decade. Accomplishers are usually reluctant to state such goals because they recognize that followers expect the great to appear humble. Nevertheless, they must be honest with themselves in order to focus properly.

People wondered why I located Philip Crosby Associates in Winter Park, Florida. I was tired of cold winters, that's why. Kaiser Wilhelm may have begun World War I because he wanted to shoot grouse on a Scottish estate, for all I know. Perhaps Thanksgiving dinner was created as a way to do a census count of the local population. The motivations of most leaders are personal and may never be known.

Each action taken during the leadership journey has an effect on the outcome of the trip. For every action there is a reaction, in leadership just as in physics. As the leader establishes the agenda of the organizational vehicle, in order to accomplish the personal agenda, this must be remembered.

THE ORGANIZATIONAL AGENDA

Organizational agendas are easier to create and display than personal agendas. Their purpose is to establish the framework within which all work is done. This agenda is for the employees, suppliers, and customers of the organization, whether it be a profit-making company, a philanthropic foundation, a Scout troop, or a religious sect. In some fashion, those involved must know where it is moving in order to do their jobs. They don't have to know everything, just enough to relate to their individual parts of the cause and effect.

*T*he first task of the leader is to define the mission.
—Peter Drucker

Winston Churchill was able to transmit the entire allied agenda for World War II by standing with his arm raised, his fingers forming a "V." Everyone knew that the goal was victory and the measurement was "unconditional surrender." Unfortunately this agenda expired with the end of the war, and people found themselves with no plans to deal with a new world.

One of the things that happens to those who take a cruise is that they are put on mailing lists for all the cruise lines. You can cruise the Amazon, go to Alaska, tour the Mediterranean or the Caribbean, or go around the world. The ships are either new or have just been overhauled. Each line searches for improved ways of creating happy customers. The competition is very spirited, and good deals can be made if one knows what one is doing.

A cruise serves as an analogy for a discussion of the clear agenda for an organization. The brochure for a cruise line lists all the places its vessels will travel during the

UPI/Bettmann

During World War II, Sir Winston Churchill inspired the people of Great Britain by making the "V for victory" sign at every opportunity.

An agenda enables people to coordinate what they are expected to do.

coming year. One trip is from San Francisco to Hawaii, Australia, South Africa, India, Malaysia, Singapore, Hong Kong, China, Korea, Japan, and back to San Francisco. The listing is complete in every detail, e.g., the ship will dock in Bombay at 8 A.M. on the 16th of March, and passengers will have a full day of touring, have lunch at the Raj hotel, and depart at 6 P.M. that evening. Those events are going to happen months from the date the brochure was printed.

By looking at this cruise agenda, the employees of the line, its suppliers, and its customers know what is supposed to take place and when, and are able to do their agreed part in making it happen. While the passengers are reclining in deck chairs anticipating lunch, the crew is preparing a menu that was designed months before, just prior to the food in the recipes being scheduled to be purchased. The serving people on the ship have been recruited, trained, and scheduled. Port officials, tour companies, and limousine companies around the world have been notified of the ship's schedule.

All of this relates to the importance of the leader's agenda. Everyone involved in meeting the leader's goals needs to know what is going to happen and when. All have to know their personal parts in the interconnected operations.

Few leaders are in a position to issue a four-color brochure concerning the agenda they visualize for the organization. They have to devise other ways of presenting it. The first level of presentation is a slogan or set of statements that presents the leader's objective in terms that everyone can grasp. For example, the political leader of an emerging nation might state: "A chicken in every pot." It doesn't take a lot of imagination to work out that placing a chicken in every pot would require a lot of chickens and a distribution system to deliver them to the pots. More than that, the leader is making a statement about general prosperity: that citizens will be able to place chickens in their pots when they wish.

STATING THE AGENDA

In the business world, a leader needs to be able to relate the complete agenda in just a few sentences that can be worked into every speaking opportunity. These sentences must be clear, and the goals must be measurable.

> ### Promote a Vision
>
> **Followers need a clear idea of where you're leading them, and they need to understand why that goal is valuable to them. Your job as a leader is to provide that vision.**[1]

One problem many political leaders have had is that those who worked closely with them did not understand what they were for or against. The higher they rose, the less they seemed to commit to one policy or another. Yet those who emerged as truly great leaders had principles from which they never budged. Their agendas were clear:

- ♦ "We shall never surrender"
- ♦ "Equal rights are for everyone"
- ♦ "Special interests will not run this country"
- ♦ "The union comes first"
- ♦ "Millions for defense, not one cent for tribute"

The leader needs to put the agenda into three or four sentences and repeat them over and over until everyone has them memorized. For example, when I was heading quality for ITT, I went around saying:

- ♦ "We need to make ITT the standard for quality worldwide."
- ♦ "Zero defects is our performance standard; prevention is our concentration."

♦ "Our price of nonconformance must be reduced by 20 percent each year."

These are all understandable and measurable. They could be worked into every conversation, speech, interview, and work project. I didn't let people talk me into changing or modifying them in order to meet a current situation. There is no acceptable reason for accomplishing less than one's absolute best.

Motorola was founded on the principle of product and leadership renewal. From push-button car radios, two-way radios, and televisions, the company diversified into semiconductors, microchips, and wireless pager and cellular phone technology. Over the past fifteen years, Motorola has invested billions in new products and markets and global expansion. In 1994, its profits rose to more than $1.5 billion on sales of $22.2 billion.[2]

CREATING THE PLAN

Behind the agenda, there must be a carefully thought-out plan that implements the agenda. For example, let us assume that an organizational agenda is "A return on assets of at least 15 percent, revenues per employee over $155,000 annually, zero customer complaints, twenty new products or services launched each year, and corporate growth of 8 percent annually."

To accomplish a return of 15 percent on assets, it is necessary to have those assets invested in products and services that produce the proper revenues and high margins. This makes it necessary to take a hard look at those things that do not realize that kind of return.

So the first step is to separate the revenue-producing areas into those that are never going to reach that performance level, those that could with the correct investment of time or money, and those that are meeting or exceeding it now. Those that cannot meet it must be replaced by things that can. This sort of rotation becomes a regular part of organizational life.

Many caretaker leaders fall in love with their products or markets and hang on to them with the hope that something will change enough to produce a proper return. For this reason, many large organizations do not accomplish their potential.

REFLECTIONS

The accomplisher's personal agenda consists of long-range goals and short-term strategies and objectives. The career path of the accomplisher is not left to chance.

In personal life and in organizations, for each action there is a reaction

The organizational agenda establishes the framework within which all work is done. Employees know what is to be done, when it is to be done, and their part in making it happen.

♦ A slogan or set of statements presents the leader's agenda in terms that everyone can grasp.

♦ The leader must be able to state the agenda in a few sentences that can be worked into every speaking opportunity.

♦ The goals stated in the agenda must be understandable and measurable.

Behind the agenda, there must be a carefully thought-out plan to implement the agenda. Revenue-producing areas must be examined, and those that cannot meet the stated goals must be replaced by things that can. This sorting process becomes a regular part of organizational life.

♦ A leader needs to have a pragmatic and understandable operating philosophy.

♦ The framework of an operating philosophy is created from learning, innovating, and deciding.

Absolute 2:
A Personal
Philosophy

Leadership cannot really be taught. It can only be learned.

Harold Geneen, CEO, ITT

3

Creating a Philosophy

A leader needs to have a pragmatic and understandable operating philosophy; otherwise, it all has to be created each day. People do not like to work for, buy from, or supply those who are indecisive or uninformed.

The framework of an operating philosophy is created from learning, innovating, and deciding. We fabricate the framework, learn how to operate it, and then continuously construct more and better compartments.

Learning

When I was young, I thought that everyone knew everything and I was the only one who lived in ignorance. So if I read a statistic that didn't seem right to me, I assumed that I didn't understand. Then one day I found a book called *How to Lie with Statistics*, by Darell Huff.[2]

The business desert is layered with the bones of those who felt they understood completely and stopped learning.[1]

It pointed out that there are three kinds of averages: mean, median, and mode. One can select the average that makes one's point. The book was a complete enlightenment to me. I learned not to trust charts in which the bottom line is something other than zero, like the one on the front page of *The Wall Street Journal*. I learned that people gain their impressions from the visual image of a graph, rather than from the numbers. I learned that many statistics have a built-in bias, slanted to prove a point. I learned that everything was not necessarily what it was supposed to be.

BOOKS

Stephen Potter's books on "Gamesmanship" and "Lifemanship"[3] were clever foolishness, but along with "Parkinson's Law,"[4] about work expanding to fill the time allowed for its completion, got me excited. I realized that I had unconsciously accepted the conventional wisdom that existed in all businesses: that those who had been there longer knew most about the business, that those who were higher up in the organization were the smartest, and that all the stuff being done was very important. Implied in all this was the agreement that it was being accomplished in the best possible way. I began to see that this was not so. If nothing else, we spent a fortune doing things over. It became apparent that I could have a hand in changing the world to suit me and that if I handled it properly I could be well-rewarded in the process.

Once my eyes were opened, I became obsessed with a search for information from which to generate ideas. I found that history and the biographies of successful people were the best sources, along with books and articles written about failed operations.

I never had much use for case histories of success as learning tools. They are mostly strategy based and, unlike biographies, do not present what people really think.

The Folklore of Management, by Clarence B. Randall,[5] former chairman of Inland Steel, told me that no one in power paid any attention to those who were not. As a result, customers, workers, and shareholders had nothing to say about what went on in a business. Mythology ruled, rather than logic.

In Henry Ford's autobiography, *My Life and Work*,[6] I learned that conventional business beliefs are usually not founded on common sense. Ford pointed out, for instance, that "having a stock of raw materials or finished goods in excess of requirements is waste which like every other waste turns up in high prices and low wages." In 1926, Ford practiced what is now known as that wonderful Japanese invention of "just-in-time inventory." Also, although Ford did not invent the automobile, he did realize that he could learn to build cars for a few hundred dollars each and sell millions of them. That brought on the assembly line and the automobile dealer.

I began to study the views of economists and the reality of economics.

> *The leader must know, must know that he knows, and must be able to make it abundantly clear to those about him that he knows.*
>
> —Clarence B. Randall

From the collections of Henry Ford Museum & Greenfield Village

Henry and Edsel Ford reviewing the one millionth Ford V-8, Ford assembly line, 1934.

I read Will Durant's ten-volume history of civilization,[7] lugging those big books on airplanes for years. I devoured his *Story of Philosophy*.[8] Accepting the philosophers as business mentors changed my whole outlook. They seemed very up to date; their wisdom reached out over the years. For example, Aristotle described the ideal executive:

> He does not speak evil of others, even of his enemies, unless it be to themselves. His carriage is sedate, his voice deep, his speech measured; he is not given to hurry, for he is concerned about only a few things; he is not prone to vehemence and bears the accidents of life with dignity and grace, making the best of his circumstances....is his own best friend and takes delight in privacy whereas the man of no virtue or ability is his own worst enemy.

Aristotle predicted the fate of communism when he wrote, "When everyone owns everything no one will

Stock Montage

Aristotle teaching Alexander the Great

take care of anything." That led me to always be absolutely certain that someone was specifically in charge of each task. After awhile, everyone knew that it was part of my operating philosophy. When I wanted to know how something was going, it was necessary to ask only one person, not a committee or team.

Voltaire thought that education would change people for the better; Rosseau thought that the old institutions had to be torn down before anyone could make a permanent change. As one who tried to educate senior management in quality for thirty years without much success, I have to say that Rosseau seems to prevail in this matter. It wasn't until their companies were in mortal danger from quality-minded competition that managers began to listen. From that lesson, I have learned to speak to top management only when it is possible to put a number in every sentence.

Newspapers and Magazines

Through reading, I have discovered that the past holds a treasure trove of ideas that can incite me to innovate. They come together with contemporary life as I read newspapers and magazines. I study *The New York Times, The Wall Street Journal, The Financial Times,* and the local newspaper each day. If I travel out of the country and cannot get them, they are saved at home, and I catch up on my return. I don't read them so much for the news but to notice trends of life and to discover when new thinking might begin to be accepted.

Business and news magazines such as *Fortune, Forbes, Business Week,* and *The Economist,* are very helpful in helping a leader to develop a personal philosophy.

It is other people's experience that makes the older man wiser than the younger man.

—Yoruba proverb

If you prepare yourself at every point as well as you can, with whatever means you have...you will be able to grasp opportunity for broader experience when it appears. Without preparation you cannot do it.

—Eleanor Roosevelt

Because I deal with people, I also skim through *The New Yorker, Vanity Fair, New York, Departures, Art and Antiques, Travel and Leisure, Atlantic,* and *Harpers,* and I flip though my wife's magazines when they are lying around. It doesn't take much effort to do this, especially if you look selectively.

It didn't take me long to discover that a lot of people do not have an interest in reading and learning. Many people seem to be satisfied with what they already know. I had a boss who read only *Newsweek* and listened only to the six o'clock news. He was brain dead at the age of forty.

WORKERS

Using one's learning is what makes life successful. When it comes to the application of information, everyone can teach us something, even if it is negative. Whenever I visit an organization, I make certain that I speak with the workers, particularly if there is a problem under consideration. Usually, they know the problem even if the solution is not available to them.

Years ago, in Spain, the ITT telephone plant was having trouble with failing receiver capsules—the ones that fit inside the ear pieces on telephones. These random failures were found to be due to microscopic contamination. The workers pointed out to me that there was another company down the road and that it emitted debris. The solution I suggested to local management was to build a dirt-free room for assembling the receivers. Neither the management nor the workers had ever seen or heard about one of these rooms. I was very familiar with them, of course, since we also had semiconductor plants in the United States. So, between us, we knew enough to arrive at the solution. We invited a company expert on such rooms to come over and advise the Spanish operation. It all worked out very well.

According to the American Quality Foundation, a New York think tank, 70% of U.S. workers are afraid to speak up with suggestions or to ask for clarification.[9]

If a person with broad knowledge and experience can be combined with people who can describe the problem, there is a synergism that creates innovation.

MENTORS AND EXAMPLES

My bosses at the Martin-Marietta company thirty years ago, Jim Halpin and Tom Willey, showed me how an executive could take charge of what had become a slipshod operation and shape it up quickly. Willey did it by leadership and example, Halpin by policies and procedures.

> Talk to people, visit other offices and work sites, ask questions, and observe how business is being handled. Often you will gain new insights into your work and find new opportunities for motivating your followers.[10]

Faced with an unhappy and nervous work force, Willey started opening the large missile plant for special dinner and tour evenings. Workers were invited to bring their spouses, have dinner with all the managers, and then take their spouses on tours and show them what went on all day. Senior executives were directed to show up and be pleasant. This helped managers and employees to get to know one another better and generated greater respect among them.

In the same manner, participating in the open-management system at ITT—set up by Harold Geneen—let me learn from every kind of situation. Executives were forced to lay it all out on the table for all to see or suffer failure by themselves when their sins (inevitably) were discovered. No exposure meant no help. By watching what people did right and wrong and by helping them to snatch victory from the jaws of defeat, I was able to gain a great deal of experience. I learned that no problem was so unimportant that it could be permitted to fester.

The most important element in establishing a happy, prosperous atmosphere was an insistence upon open, free, and honest communications up and down the ranks of our management structure.

—Harold Geneen

Experience is not what happens to you; it is what you do with what happens to you.
—Aldous Huxley

CLIENTS

In Philip Crosby Associates, I learned from my clients. As we taught them about quality management, they showed us their businesses. Most of the time, those who were running the client organizations were very good teachers.

Leaders must learn vigorously and from every source. Don't block off anything.

INNOVATING

Innovation comes from learning firmly pressed up against need. To generate new ideas and ways of doing things, we have to challenge ourselves.

Most people will work very hard to understand the systems of their organizations, e.g., how a reservation is processed. Newcomers are expected to master the old ways whether they make sense or not. However, if we learn to look at things in terms of the result that is needed—rather than the system being used to produce that result—we can innovate on command. Patching is not innovating.

On overseas business trips, I complain that I have to wear a jacket while traveling in order to have enough pockets to handle the paperwork involved (tickets, passports, custom's declarations, and such). Why can't the airline give me a little plastic card with an encoded magnetic strip on the other side? It could contain all the information anyone needs. Subways in the U.S., England, and Hong Kong use such cards. Surely, someone is working on this innovation right now.

Carl Ally says that the creative person wants to be a know-it-all. He wants to know about all kinds of things: ancient history, 19th century mathematics, current manufacturing techniques, flower arranging, and hog futures. Because he never knows when these ideas might come together to form a new idea. It may happen six minutes later or six months or six years down the road. But he has faith that it will happen.[11]

Many who would innovate become tangled in the webs of systems and approaches. I once was asked to help a CEO reorganize a company in preparation for an expansion. She laid the organizational chart on a table, and we studied it for about ten minutes. She told me that she wanted to create a very efficient and helpful staff. When she asked me what I thought, I suggested that we turn the chart over. The other side was blank. She gazed at it for a few moments and then smiled. "What a wonderful idea," she said. She wrote down exactly what she needed and then fitted people into that as best she could. Those who no longer fit would be dealt with justly. It was done that way, and the place runs well.

To innovate, it is necessary to state the result desired and to define it as clearly as possible. What would you like to see happen? Guests coming in the lobby of your hotel and going straight to their rooms without having to check in at the front desk? Insurance customers writing their own policies? New employees trained quickly and well? The ideas will flow free and fast if we learn what has happened in the past and mix that with what is available now. For example, we would not have all the telephone wires and poles if someone could have sold the cellular phone technology when it originated years ago.

> **I**n the future, tiny radio transmitters embedded in credit cards may reveal the identities of shoppers as they walk in the store or the department.[12]

AWARDS PROGRAMS

The motivational aspects of the leader's personal philosophy should be disseminated to all in the organization. A good way to do this is through awards programs. There are several points to be made regarding awards. First, it is not a good idea to give awards to companies, because they think they are finished when they receive them. Individuals think it is time to work harder.

I wanted to have "quality" awards at ITT to recognize the individuals who were producing real quality work. I knew that most awards generate a great deal of trouble from those who do not receive them. This raises the second point: incentive programs have a very poor success record, because they tend to work in the opposite direction. The people who receive the awards are happy, but everybody else is upset or demotivated.

The key seems to be the selection of winners and the value of the award. I thought that we should have peer nomination and that the award should be a ring for men, a medallion for women. The only restrictions were that no one could nominate his or her boss and that I was not eligible. We took the resulting nominations each year, sorted them, and recognized everyone. About twenty awards were presented each year by the president of the company at a wonderful dinner. The other nominees received silver pins and certificates at luncheons in their own divisions. This recognition program has been going on for over twenty years, and no one has complained about a winner yet. The company

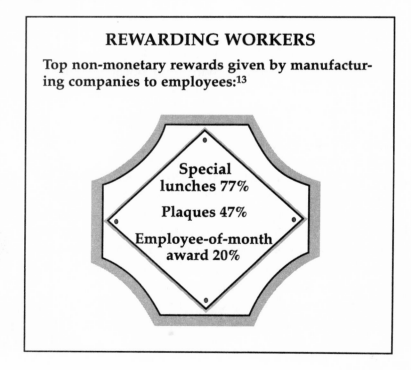

REWARDING WORKERS

Top non-monetary rewards given by manufacturing companies to employees:[13]

Special lunches 77%

Plaques 47%

Employee-of-month award 20%

has had the benefit of the winners being examples of quality all those years. They inspire everyone around them.

On the other hand, when government branches and associations develop award systems that require companies to nominate themselves, questions are almost always raised about the integrity of the programs.

*T*ake *time to deliberate, but when the time for action has arrived, stop thinking and go in.*
—Napoleon Bonaparte

DECIDING

Learning and innovation are nothing without decision. When a leader makes a decision, it is for the purpose of taking acting on something. The decision has to describe the action that will take place and set the performance limits. Waiting for consensus usually produces a compromise and avoids the tough choices. Get the necessary input, make the decision, and then sell the decision if necessary.

Saying "yes" or "no" must be done so that it cannot be misunderstood. The Japanese have made an art out of not saying "yes" while not saying "no" either. It seems to work for them, but most other people want to know one way or another.

Above all else, a leader's decisions must be consistent. People don't mind a dumb or uninformed choice now and then, but when there is a pattern of wavering, they quickly lose respect for the leader. They do nothing when the first command arrives but wait for the inevitable counter order. Soon the work drops to a slow pace; morale drops; and everyone, including the leader, becomes more frustrated.

*S*helving *hard decisions is the least ethical course.*
—Adrian Cadbury,
Chairman, Cadbury
Schweppes

Those who are dedicated to continuous learning, who know how the world works; who keep their eyes on results rather than on systems, and who are willing to make decisions clearly and firmly are the ones who will command.

REFLECTIONS

The framework of an operating philosophy is created from learning, innovating, and deciding.

LEARNING:

- ♦ Reading can help one to learn what is not true as well as what is.

- ♦ Learning is not enough; it is using what one learns that makes one successful in life.

- ♦ Be absolutely certain that someone is specifically in charge of every task. That way, when you want to know what is going on, you have to ask only one person.

- ♦ Workers often can identify the problem, even if they do not know the solution.

INNOVATING:

- ♦ Innovation comes from learning firmly pressed up against need.

- ♦ If we learn to look at things in terms of the result that is needed—rather than the system being used to produce that result—we can innovate.

- ♦ The motivational aspects of the leader's philosophy should be disseminated to all.

DECIDING:

- ♦ Learning and innovation are nothing without decision.

- ♦ The decision has to describe the action that will take place and set performance limits.

♦ Organizational life consists of transactions and relationships.

♦ The key to enduring relationships is respect.

♦ A good relationship takes thought.

ABSOLUTE 3: ENDURING RELATIONSHIPS

How much grief could be avoided if everyone at the workplace simply practiced a bit of consideration and courtesy!

Andrew S. Grove, CEO, Intel Corp.

4

RELATIONSHIPS CANNOT BE LEFT TO CHANCE

Getting along with others in the right way is the hardest part of life. The key is respect for the other person, nation, race, culture, or whatever is involved. History, both personal and social, is about the conflict that results from lack of respect.

There are changing relationships in all aspects of life. We as individuals relate to some people some of the time and to some people never. We form paths of familiar activities that include those we like or need and we change those paths as we move through our lives. About half the marriages these days end in divorce. Old friends move away, and new friends are made. Organizations join one another in work with varied results.

Life is not so short but that there is always time enough for courtesy.

—Ralph Waldo Emerson

In later chapters, I go into detail about relationships with customers, suppliers, employees, bosses, and family members. In this chapter, I introduce the concept of relationships to make certain we have a common understanding of what is involved.

Relationships cannot be left to chance. Organizational life consists of transactions and relationships. If we are going to send someone something, or do something for someone, we have to have a relationship. This means we must know the other party in a positive way, and that requires some work. There is a courtship, a romance, and a continuing involvement. A good relationship takes thought.

The thoughtful, relationship-oriented person in an organization may not always be the one with the most important title on the door or the one who dominates meetings. It may not even be the person to whom others turn for action. But in every successful organization there is at least one person who is oriented toward relationships and who guides others. The official leader does well to identify and encourage this person. The following story illustrates this.

THE EXAMPLE OF THE BANK MERGER

When a large bank took over a small bank recently, it was anxious to make a good impression on the customers of the acquired bank. The intent was to encourage them to stay where they were rather than go to other banks that were soliciting their business.

The operations staff prepared a booklet that explained the large bank; it listed many of the service options that had not been offered by the small bank. As part of the package, the bank people included a questionnaire. Its intent was to gain information to help the bank serve the customers better. The data would be put into the computer system and would be available for marketing analyses. The complete package would weigh four ounces and would be sent first class. The president thought it was a great idea, the marketing director was delighted, and the operations staff could hardly wait to get its hands on the data to be generated from the returned forms.

Ellen Hamsveld, the treasurer, listened to the marketing presentation about the "welcome package." She then said that she thought that receiving this bundle in the mail would cause many customers to move their business to a bank that would not "bug" them.

"They already know that we are a big, complex bank that has taken over their little, personal bank," she said. "All this will just make them think that we are going to hassle them like big banks do. Why do you think they did business with the little bank when there are three big banks in town?"

*T*act, respect, and generosity toward variant views will always commend themselves....

—Felix Frankfurter, U.S. Supreme Court Justice

"What do you suggest we do?," asked the president.

Ellen shrugged. "I would send them a postcard that says something like: 'Welcome to your new bank. Please drop by and say hello so we can make certain we are serving you properly. We are glad to be here.' I'm sure you could punch it up better than that."

There was a long silence. The marketing team looked dejected, and the president was pensive.

"Why do you think they will respond negatively to this package?" asked the marketing director. "We were thinking that they would like to know more about their bank, and we do have several options that were not available to them before. We can offer them flexible loans, free checking, bill paying, and trust services that they didn't have with the old bank."

"Yet they did business with the old bank," said Ellen. "If we want to build a relationship with them, we have to do a little courting first. Shoving a package at them is not the way to open a conversation. There is plenty of time for them to learn about the financial tools we can offer."

"Did you ever come to this bank before we acquired it?" she asked. "There was never anyone inside. The lobby was almost always empty, but the drive-through was busy, and the ATM had a continual stream of users. People arranged their automobile loans and such by phone. In the past eight years, the small bank had only one nonperforming loan."

"So, Ellen," the President said, "You think we should 'court' the customers a little rather than coming on strong? How long does the courtship take?"

"A lot less than building a whole new string of customers," she replied. "Right now, relationships between the bank and its customers are very good. The touch is light on both sides. The bank has attracted people who use money as a tool and don't need a lot of help. We might want to take advantage of that in order to grow in that direction."

The marketing director sighed. "I think you have something here, Ellen. But we do need to let them know they are now in a more advantageous situation. How about if we send the postcard or letter you suggested and include an invitation to drop by the bank and pick up a package if they want to?"

"We could also give them a number to call so we could mail the package to them," said the president. "That way it would be at their request."

And that is what the bank did. Many customers did ask for the package, and none left the bank in order to escape the evils of "bigness." Over a period of time, each customer was informed about the options available, and the revenue per client of the bank grew. There was a good relationship.

> ## REFLECTIONS
>
> ♦ To maintain a relationship, we have to know the other party in a positive way, and that takes work.
>
> ♦ Relationships involve courtship and continuing involvement. This applies to relationships with significant others, friends, peers, coworkers, subordinates, suppliers, and customers or clients.
>
> ♦ In every successful organization there is at least one person who is oriented toward relationships and who guides others. The leader does well to identify and encourage this person.

Being "worldly" means knowing how to deal with:

♦ Other cultures

♦ Technology

♦ The gathering of information

ABSOLUTE 4: WORLDLY

A *"Copernican revolution" must take place in the attitudes of American CEOs as the international economy no longer revolves around the U.S. and the world market is shared by many strong players.*

Lester Korn

5

AN EXAMPLE OF BEING WORLDLY

Fred Bigley looked up as Susan Meyers walked into his office. Rising from his chair, Fred shook hands with Susan and asked, "How was the trip? Apparently you got to India and back in good shape."

Susan smiled and took a little wooden figure from her briefcase, presenting it to Fred. "Here is a good-luck piece, hand made from sandalwood. I bought it just for you at the Taj Mahal the day before yesterday."

Fred admired the piece. "Thank you," he said. "That was most considerate. The workmanship is excellent. Are you sure you want to spend all this money on me?"

The international-al market is more than four times larger than the U.S. market. Growth rates in many overseas markets far outpace domestic market growth.[1]

"I spare no expense for my colleagues," Susan replied. "It cost me two dollars, and my Indian friend says I paid too much."

The two sat down, and Fred lifted a few papers from his desk. "I really appreciate receiving your report so quickly," he said. "How did you make that happen?"

Susan lifted her briefcase off the floor and waved it at Fred. "Through the magic of my laptop. Instead of snail mail, we have E-mail. I just wrote it out and zapped it to you via the telephone plug in my hotel room. Using the overseas charge card, I was able to do it at a very low cost, too."

"Well, as a result, we were able to take the correct position before any of the competition, so we are in good shape on this particular deal. How about the rest of the trip? Did you have any problem with traveling, or hotels, or food, or anything?"

Susan smiled and shook her head. "Not a bit. I planned the whole thing in advance, like I always do. The reservations came through just as agreed. I had read up on India and talked with some people who had lived there as expatriates. This made it easier for me to adapt. Something like that is particularly important when it comes to food. I enjoy Indian food but I didn't know that until we tried it before leaving.

"Also, I stopped over in London on the way, which let me check out the status with our folks there. I was able to wander the streets a bit, see a show, and get myself in shape for the rest of the flights."

© Bruce Ayres / Tony Stone Images

Travel and technology are major aspects of the global economy.

Fred shook his head. "How do you manage that? I am always completely tied up during my trips. There is no time to do anything. I come back exhausted."

Susan wagged a finger at Fred. "I've been trying to expose you to some reason on this travel business. It is necessary to become comfortable with it; after all, we will be doing it for a number of years. The world is one big office now. Until recently, 90 percent of our business was conducted in the U.S. and Europe. Within a few years, the rest of the world will be our main customers. We will have to learn how to deal with them there and here. Part of that is in the art of traveling."

One-fourth of U.S. business loans come from foreign sources.[2]

"So tell me," said Fred, "What did you do?"

"When I am facing some time-zone changes, like going to London, I leave on Friday evening. That puts me in my hotel on Saturday morning, and I sleep to around noon. Then I go out into the daylight; that helps with the time change. I wander around and have a meal in a comfortable spot. Then I take a brief nap and bath and go to the theater, walking all the way.

"On Sunday, I do tourist things, wherever I am. It is a great way to get comfortable with the city and the country. I wandered around New Delhi. In India, I was in the company of people who were able to lead me around, and I learned a lot. Sometimes Ben can go with me, and I have learned to arrange 'companion tickets' with the airlines."

"How do you keep up with what is happening everywhere? I read all the newspapers and magazines but keep being surprised," noted Fred.

"I get *The London Financial Times* daily at home and *The Economist* magazine weekly. They cover the world. I get the *Asian Wall Street Journal* and a couple of newsletters from India and Indonesia. Between them, it is possible to get an overview, but it would take a full-time commitment to keep up with the whole

Information by itself is not knowledge; it requires the addition of experience and consideration.

world. I think we need our own news-gathering group. We should talk about that at the next general management meeting."

Susan obviously has learned how to travel and deal with people in other parts of the world. That is the key to being "worldly." She has learned to deal with other cultures, with technology, and with the gathering of information. She also knows that information by itself is not knowledge; it requires the addition of experience and consideration. She thinks in terms of the world economy, along with the need to act locally. She reads magazines and newspapers from foreign sources and has friends around the world. She has learned what to eat and what to avoid. You will find bottled water at her side, even at home. She doesn't drink alcohol while traveling because she knows that it dehydrates her and hinders recuperation from jet lag.

In short, Susan is "worldly," in a business sense. Customers, suppliers, colleagues, and employees are everywhere. Susan treats everyone with respect. She is unerringly polite and considerate. She knows how to get things done in many cultures. She knows that it is not necessary to understand the details of other cultures, only to respect them.

REFLECTIONS

◆ Being worldly means being able to utilize new technological advances.

◆ Being worldly means having an understanding of one's global marketplace.

◆ Being worldly means learning about and showing respect for the people, customs, conditions, and business practices of the places in which one will be doing business.

◆ Being worldly means knowing how to travel effectively.

◆ Being worldly means staying informed of what is happening in the global arena and, in particular, having up-to-date information about the areas in which one does business.

♦ Money is nourishment for an organization, not medicine.

♦ It is more important to prevent financial problems than to know how to solve them.

♦ Debt removes options.

♦ Financial measurement systems should be understood and implemented by all involved.

THE LEADER AND FINANCE

---

*The distribution of wealth depends on the laws
and customs of society.*

John Stuart Mill

6

FINANCIAL LEADERSHIP

In business life—and personal life, too—there is constant
variation in the economic integrity of the enterprise.
However, a financially well-managed organization
does not suffer such ups and downs to the degree that
others do.

It is necessary for a leader to understand the various aspects of finance. The most important thing is to
deal with reality, not with custom. Leaders have to recognize that an organization is a body and money is its
nourishment, not a form of control. Money does not
make things happen, it only provides the fuel. A lot of it
can be used up making useless bonfires or warming
empty buildings.

The Small
Business
Administration
estimates that up
to 75% of new
businesses fail
during the first
few years of
operation.[1]

START UPS

Writing a business plan, whether for a start-up or for a continuing enterprise, brings out the fairy dust in people. They imagine that others have the same level of interest in the product or service as they do. An imagined revenue stream is laid out, and then expenses are assigned to absorb it.

When a start-up group does manage to raise the money it needs, the scenario usually is that it follows the plan exactly, manages the money carefully, and spends it all. It arrives at the end of the plan with no product, no customers, and no company.

At least once a month, I am asked to meet with a budding entrepreneur who has a business plan that cannot fail. The plan requires a certain amount of money—usually well over a million dollars—and lays out a complete strategy. The entrepreneur is going to rent offices, hire staff, select a marketing director, and do some additional research.

I always ask if the business has any customers yet and suggest that everything be taken out of the plan that does not deal with actually delivering the product or service to the customers. After the business has sold something and has a cash flow, the entrepreneur can look into acquiring offices and a staff. That usually ends the discussion, but many of the entrepreneurs call me later to say that they wished they had taken my advice or they did take it and things worked out well.

It is better to take over and build upon an existing business than to start a new one.

—Harold Geneen

TURNING AROUND A BUSINESS

The best leadership role now is turning around companies that have failed. Turn arounds shouldn't take longer than a year. The key is to find out what is wrong with the organization, and the employees will tell you that. Where leaders get into trouble is asking the existing managers for advice. If they knew what to do they would have done it. Get rid of them. Hire people you trust, regardless of what they cost. Get rid of all the activities that the old management loved but could not justify. Cash in the company plane and fly business class. Change the culture.

MONEY IS A TOOL, NOT A PRODUCT

Any jackass can draw up a balanced budget on paper.
—Lane Kirkland,
President, AFL-CIO

In over forty years, I have never seen any real company money, just numbers on paper. It is easy to forget that those figures represent something. People can lose respect for something that does not appear to exist. Thus, respect for money has to be imprinted in everyone's mind.

Money should be spent only in a way that helps the organization to grow and prosper, preferably on something that will grow in value. The "way" is not always obvious; a great deal of money routinely is expended with the best of intentions on things that will never make any difference.

Many opportunities that seem like good ideas at the time fade as more information develops. Companies and nations have learned the hard way, for instance, that borrowing money in order to fulfill a grand plan usually ends with a large debt and little gain. This is why very few mergers actually succeed; the debt involved removes many options from management. It has to manage twice as effectively as the previous group in order to break even. In addition, this burden of debt means the company or nation cannot always meet the initiatives of competitors, such as cutting prices on short notice.

When a leader wants an organization to conform to a vision, it is vital to have a firm hand on finances. This means knowing where the money originates and where it has gone in the past and directing the flow into the things that make the vision happen. Doing this successfully requires three things:

1. Understanding the concept of money as nourishment rather than as medicine.
2. Preventing financial problems.
3. Making measurements understood and implemented by all involved.

MONEY AS NOURISHMENT

Most of us can see that money has been expended on us in different ways over the years. Many things that at one time were vital to our existence (diapers, baby food) were replaced by school expenses, play clothes, summer camp, orthodontics, and the accoutrements of childhood. Then came dressy clothes, a car, college, and an apartment with furnishings. Marriage may have brought back a relationship with diapers and a entirely new line of expenses, many of which had not been appreciated or even known before.

CHANGING NEEDS

The activities that require nourishment in our personal lives change continually, and we have to rearrange our lives to accommodate reality. However, most business organizations do not respond in that way. Spending money on specific things becomes embedded in the operation. The fact that the things might not be needed does not enter into the situation.

That also is the way in which governments operate. They have diaper-

The people who get into trouble in our company are those who carry around the anchor of the past.

—Jack Welch, CEO, General Electric

service purchasing functions even when everyone is potty-trained. The function never goes away because the expenditure represents someone's job. Unless something replaces it, it will never change.

The typical executive does not accept change willingly, which makes the leadership role more difficult. Organizations traditionally are structured around budgets assigned to departments. Great consideration is given to planning future expenses, and much argument is expended on how much to raise or lower the amount pledged to each operation. The question of eliminating anything rarely arises. As a result, the budget is fully committed, and when new requirements arise, it is difficult to find funds for them.

For this reason, business lore is packed with stories of individuals who had to overcome all objections in order to bring their companies, industries, or even countries into a new age. From Fulton and his steamboat to me out peddling quality to the uninterested, this is the way in which much progress has come about.

*T*he budget evolved from a management tool into an obstacle to management.

—Frank C. Carlucci, U.S. Secretary of Defense

Computers are not used properly because of reluctance to spend money on software that cannot be seen; research in unexplored areas suffers due to lack of definition. Every thinking person knows of a place in his or her organization where large sums of money could be saved if only a little bit were expended on a new way of doing things. Unfortunately, people usually have no way of communicating such insight except to set themselves on fire in front of the board room.

Budgets are established to control, not to manage. When I was young, it was common for newly married couples to manage their money by labeling envelopes according to planned expenses. The cash sums for rent, food, entertainment, clothes, allowances, and such were neatly filed in the appropriate envelopes in the kitchen cabinet. This system invariably fell apart with the first unplanned expense. Unplanned expenses always occur. You might as well give up and include them in the budget under "unplanned."

PREVENTING FINANCIAL PROBLEMS

In financial management, one needs to concentrate on the cash flow of the organization and use it properly. This is the revenue stream that comes from selling the products and services of the company. Tributaries to that stream come from investments, depreciation, and other sources. Similar activities occur in nature.

The Colorado river, for instance, winds its way out of the Rocky Mountains into Southern California and Arizona. Each drop of water is committed to do some-

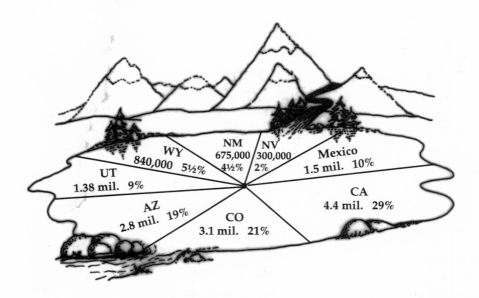

Allocations of water from the Colorado River. Total annual flow = 15 million acre feet. 1 acre foot = 326,000 gallons.

thing for someone. The stream is treasured, controlled, measured, and fought over. Sometimes when the winter snows are not up to standard, the water flow subsides. Then someone has to suffer. The river has been over-pledged for years, and unless someone can figure out how to increase its water sources by a significant amount, the lack of water is always going to disappoint a lot of people.

Increasing capacity by acquiring more rivers to add to the supply is not realistic (beside, it would only add to the requirements that the system must meet). The next best step is to concentrate on expending the water for the most important reasons. There are vast areas that receive a majority of the water for irrigation, much of it for crops that are far from essential. They are nourished only because of some prior arrangement—political, social, or legal. For the most part, farmers receive the water at little or no expense to them. To resolve the problem, some hard decisions need to be made, based on a set of agreed priorities.

In every company and family, this situation exists. There are traditional and other long-standing arrangements in which funds are committed that no longer have clear meaning. Resources could better be put into something that will grow. The vision of the leader has to be spelled out so clearly that these areas become obvious to everyone.

To prevent causing financial problems for ourselves, we have to work within the cash flow of the organization. We have to make certain that everyone understands what it means to respect assets and revenues. People must learn to attend to corporate nourishment with the same seriousness they give to personal nourishment.

The bankruptcies the business magazines write about are almost always preventable. Basic prevention usually comes down to not spending—or committing to spend—more than you are going to receive. That sounds

According to William C. McGowan, Chairman of MCI, "The only thing that matters is cash flow—not the cash flows they use today, but the old cash flows that laid out the source and application of funds—where it's coming from and where it's going and how much is left over. No company has ever gone bankrupt because it had a loss on its P&L."

simple, but few do it. We need to avoid the obvious black holes of debt and overexpansion. We need clear policies that prohibit us from doing things we cannot pay for out of the current cash flow.

MAKING MEASUREMENTS UNDERSTOOD AND USED BY ALL

Conventional financial-measurement systems are usually not effective because they are budget related, behind the time curve, and subject to managerial manipulation. Organizations with exotic reporting and analysis methods are still being surprised by unexpected results. If a leader is going to use finances properly, they must be measured and reported in a form that ordinary people can understand. This requires an accounting system based on reality rather than on custom.

To reiterate, budgets do not lead to good financial management. To invest time at the beginning of the year allocating funds to different functions and projects, and then spend the rest of the year seeing if the money is spent, is not financial management. It is manipulation. For one thing, the cleverest managers often get the biggest budgets. Being honest is not the way to get ahead in a budget-driven organization.

The reason budgeters prevail is that many senior managers do not want to make decisions about where money should go. They like consensus; they do not want to establish priorities. They do not feel strongly enough about their visions for their organizations.

Yet when a leader does establish priorities, everyone is thrilled. People want direction, they like to know what is important. This does not make them into "yessers," it relieves them of game playing so they can get to work.

The management team can allocate the funds available in the cash flow in order to run the organization the best way to meet the vision. "Allocations," not "budgets," have results-oriented, measurable targets. You can know what you are getting for your money.

This way the organization can measure its financial status in a straightforward manner. How much revenue have we received? How much have we spent for compensation? Benefits? Research and development? Human resources? Quality? Project 326? Project 112? Accounts receivable and payable?

The leader needs to make certain that the person in charge of managing this system knows what he or she is doing. It is imperative to have an excellent comptroller and a computer system with appropriate software so that real-time financial analysis is available. Have this system installed in your own office and interrogate it continually. When expenses or revenues are not what they should be, find out what is happening, right then. Do not wait for the monthly report; a project can bleed to death by then.

> *Whenever parameters can be quantified, it is usually desirable to do so.*
>
> —Norman R. Augustine,
> President and CEO,
> Martin Marietta

Customers should be billed by computer and asked to pay by electronic transfer. The same arrangements should be made with suppliers. Cut the "float" out of the business. It will also eliminate much of the need for a credit line and other borrowing to cover inventories.

To control revenues per employee, most executives do some arithmetic and then examine the reasons there are too many employees or not enough revenue. However, a more efficient way is to start with expenses. What is the price of error? Is money being spent doing things over? Is there a proper orientation and training program for employees? Do they know what to do? Do they have the equipment to do the job? Many such things must be considered.

All this financial effort should take about a third of the leader's time. That leaves a third for quality and a third for relationships. Once everyone else realizes that the leader is aware of what is going on and cares about how the vision is implemented, they will follow the same pattern.

Working from reality rather than from custom, understanding the concept of money as nourishment, preventing financial problems, and implementing practical financial measurements, along with teaching respect for money, are the tools for a "leadership friendly" financial-management system.

REFLECTIONS

Money does not make things happen; it only provides the fuel.

Start-up business plans should focus on those things that actually deliver the product or service to the customer.

The existing managers won't be able to tell you what is wrong in an organization; if they could, they would have fixed it. Ask the workers.

People can lose respect for something that does not appear to exist. Respect for money has to be imprinted in everyone's mind.

Ways of spending money become habitual in many organizations. Conventional financial-measurement systems are usually not effective because they are budget related, behind the time curve, and subject to managerial manipulation. In most organizations, departmental budgets contain traditional expenses, some of which no longer have meaning. But the question of eliminating anything rarely arises. As a result, the budget is fully committed, and when new requirements arise, it is difficult to find funds for them.

Having a firm hand on finances means knowing where the money originates and where it has gone in the past and directing the flow into the things that will grow—that will make the vision happen. Financial priorities change continually and must be questioned regularly.

Finances must be measured and reported in a form that ordinary people can understand. This requires an accounting system that is based on reality rather than on custom.

Three things are necessary to cause quality: policy, education, and example.

The Absolutes of Quality Management are:

♦ Conformance to requirements

♦ Prevention

♦ Performance standards

♦ Measurement

THE LEADER AND QUALITY

Improve constantly and forever the system of production and service, to improve quality and productivity, and thus constantly decrease costs.

W. Edwards Deming

7

BEGINNING WITH QUALITY

Many leaders are likely to have the opportunity to change organizations that are in trouble into successful ones. There are only two actions necessary to make this happen:

1. Have the current condition well documented. Have those who want you to take the challenge note problems, revenues, profits, employee and customer turnover, inventory (if applicable), and other essentials. Document where you began, because memories are short.

2. Begin with quality.

The key is to find out where things have gone wrong for the customer and make them right. Identify and eliminate the costs of doing things wrong. Just look at the expense list, at anything that would not have to be done if there were no errors. Customer service is one of these things; the price of error is at least 25 percent of revenues.

Go see what is being given to the customers and then determine what the customers are supposed to receive. Insist that the customers be given the products and services they were promised. Recognize those who are willing to make this happen and eliminate those who think it is not possible.

THE ORGANIZATION MIRRORS THE INTEGRITY OF LEADERSHIP

I spent the early part of my career as a quality-assurance professional. My job was to protect the customer. It took me years to develop the concepts of quality management, to teach companies to "prevent." Prevention causes an organization to move from confrontation to relationships and education.

It takes real immersion for executives and managers to learn how to manage quality. This is not because they are difficult to teach; it is because they pick up so much wrong information over the years. They become confused by programs, systems, and old wives' tales.

Leaders have to accept the fact that poor management is the reason that things are not done properly in organizations. All the quality-control techniques make very little difference if management is not aimed properly. There is no need to waste time and money on "systems" such as the ISO 9000 and Baldrige. Quality is not produced by a set of books, even if they are used as guides. It comes from the leadership of the organization—most of all, from the leader personally. When attitudes are influenced in the right way, quality takes care of itself.

S trong corporate cultures, like strong family cultures, come from within, and they are built by individual leaders....[1]

SYSTEMS INTEGRITY

In the practical world of business, we need to accept one thing:

> *No organization can earn the respect*
> *and business of its customers unless it is*
> *able to deliver exactly what it said it*
> *would, every time.*

It is not enough to have a wonderful product or service if it arrives late or with errors. Customers tire quickly of excuses and disappointments. Customers want their suppliers to help them to be successful, not to provide noise in the channels.

Making customers successful means creating an organization that routinely does things right the first time. Because making this happen requires everyone's participation, I call it "systems integrity."

Systems integrity is when everything works as planned. It is the result of a carefully constructed, yet natural, operating culture. That culture cannot be purchased or packaged. It is a reflection of the leader's personal integrity.

When I was in the Navy, we were preparing to leave port one afternoon, and I overheard the captain of the ship say to the executive officer, "How do we stand, Mr. Elston?" The executive officer turned, saluted, and replied, "All systems are A-OK, sir."

Hearing this, the captain gave the order to get the ship underway, and we were off to sea.

The executive officer was reporting that every one of the systems that made the ship operate, from the engine room, to the galley, to the quartermaster, to communications, to the integrity of the hull, had been checked and found to be in proper condition. It would be foolhardy to go to sea with a leak, or without enough fuel, or without key staff members.

© *Marv Wolfe / Tony Stone Images*

Every system is checked before a Navy ship sets sail.

The leader of an organization has to make certain that all systems are A-OK when it comes to operating the organization. This applies to whatever is being managed. It does not have to be a whole corporation; it can be sales, purchasing, room service, or some other function.

When the captain asked his question, he knew that the executive officer had been checking with department heads and following up on previous situations. He knew that the executive officer continually surveyed the readiness of the ship on a moment-by-moment basis. That was done twenty-four hours a day at sea and in port. In turn, all the department heads knew exactly how their areas of responsibility stood. Below them, other supervisors and specialists were continually aware. Measurements were being taken, maintenance was being performed, corrective action was being implemented, stores were being replenished, and new people were being trained. All this action went on continually in order to be certain that the ship and crew were ready to carry out their responsibilities.

The organization's leader has to embrace systems integrity in the same manner as a ship's captain does: as something that is absolutely vital for success. This is not something that can be done for the organization by a separate group of people. It has to be accomplished by each employee and supplier as a part of normal operations. Making that happen, on a routine basis, is a primary task of the leader. Quality must be implanted, like a pacemaker; just smoothing it on has no effect.

Three actions are necessary to cause quality: policy, education, and example.

POLICY

The leader is the only one who can make quality happen.

Committees, professional quality practitioners, and government directives are useful but cause few results by themselves. Management has to make it very clear where it stands on the issue of quality. It needs to make certain that everyone in the organization and its suppliers understand that the policy is:

> We will deliver defect-free products and services, on time, to our customers and coworkers.

This policy is a direction to all employees of the organization, a promise to customers, and an agreement with suppliers. It says that each individual who is any part of the system will perform his or her tasks in the agreed manner. This policy is necessary because the world of business is traditionally oriented toward "acceptable quality levels." There are still people who think that it costs less to do things right the second time.

After this policy is generated at the highest level of the company and everyone is told about it, action has to be taken to help people conform. The importance of this cannot be overstated. If your organization has not declared a quality policy yet, issue it for your area of influence. Be a leader. Everyone will be amazed at the results.

EDUCATION

Everyone in an organization must understand how quality is defined by the organization, what orientation produces it, what performance standard applies, and what measurement should be used.

The Far Side cartoon by Gary Larsen is reprinted by permission of Chronicle Features, San Francisco, CA. All rights reserved.

And so I've reached the conclusion, gentlemen, that the Wonker Wiener Company is riddled with incompetence.

In 1991, only 10% of U.S. service companies had any kind of quality program. But it is expected that by the year 2000, 70% of those with more than 500 employees will have formal quality initiatives, according to Gunneson Group International.[2]

Education cannot be left to chance or to the training department. Just having someone stand up and talk does not change anything. It all must be tied in with people's needs.

When everyone understands quality measurement the same way, marvelous things happen. There are four things to be understood; I call them the "Absolutes of Quality Management."

Quality Absolute 1: Conformance to Requirements

Thousands of actions take place in every organization every day, for the purpose of doing the business of the organization. These actions are called "requirements."

Management's primary job is to make certain that requirements exist for every task, that the persons responsible for the job understand how to accomplish the requirements, and that the proper facilities and resources exist to accomplish the requirements.

Quality then is defined as "conforming to the requirements." That way we do what we said we were going to do. We give our customers what was promised. As we learn, we insist on continually improving the requirements and adding new ones.

If management does not specify the requirements, people will make up their own. All the plans and strategies created in the executive suite will never be implemented if they are not translated into things people can do.

If quality is defined in more traditional words such as "goodness" and "delight," no one knows what it means. Quality then becomes an "I know it when I see it" kind of thing. People will argue about how good something has to be. It is much better to have people discuss requirements and deal with specifics rather than with emotions.

Quality Absolute 2: Prevention

Prevention is the orientation for causing quality. This is opposed to the "detection" way of thinking that was used for years. Inspectors, testers, and auditors scanned the output of an operation in order to sort good from bad. It is better to create an environment in which there is no "bad," to learn how to do things right the first time. That takes prevention.

The best way I have found to understand prevention is to think of personal wellness. We all know that if we take proper preventative care of our minds and bodies, we have a better probability of living longer and in good health. However, this is something that cannot be left to chance. One might think that people would leap on this opportunity, but only a small percentage do. The problem is that we have to do all the work ourselves. It is not possible to delegate or purchase it.

The Example of the Maids. Prevention applies everywhere. For example, a hotel manager complained to me that the maids did not make up the rooms completely. There was always something left out: the room-service menu, extra towels, etc. "Just can't get good maids," she said.

Her plan was to set up a "hot line" so customers could call about their problems, and an assistant manager could run up with some towels or whatever was needed. It was going to be very expensive.

"How does one learn to make up a room?," I asked. She implied that maids were born knowing that. I disagreed and suggested that we teach them to do it her

Of 149 firms answering a questionnaire sent out by The Conference Board, 75% said that profits had increased noticeably because of lower cost and/or an increased market share resulting from higher-quality products.

PIMS Associates, Inc., correlated data collected on more than 1,000 businesses and concluded that those selling high-quality products and services were generally more profitable. They also found that both return on investment and market share rose with quality.[3]

way. She made up a room perfectly and used it to train the maids. The problem disappeared.

Quality Absolute 3: Performance Standards

For decades, people worked under the assumption that everybody makes mistakes. The orientation was toward acceptable quality levels or "that's close enough." In the 1960s, I decided that this assumption was the source of our "quality" problems. I began wondering if nurses always dropped a certain number of babies, or if people really had to have accidents each year. From there, I conceived the concept of "zero defects," which was a way of saying "do it right the first time."

"Zero defects" is the performance standard of the successful organization, not "acceptable quality levels."

Quality Absolute 4: Measurement

Executives measure everything by money, and are measured in turn by that same commodity.

It is in the area of measurement that the traditional approaches to quality fall apart. Measuring by statistics during the company's work process is valuable and should be done. However, executives measure everything by money, and are measured in turn by that same commodity. Until quality is fitted into the cash flow and displayed as an equal with the other financial considerations, it will always be an add-on. At ITT, for instance, I could never count on executive attention until we put our message in terms of money. From that point on, the executives were all eyes and ears.

No matter what organization you are involved with, you can be certain that at least 25 percent of the cash flow is spent to do work over. Repossessing, rework, nonconforming receipts from suppliers, past-due accounts receivable, and a lot of other things are handled as ordinary business. Many companies have customer-service groups that spend the majority of their time fixing the mistakes that have been inflicted on the customer.

Having the accounting department determine the price of nonconformance (error) is the best way to assure executive involvement. The price of nonconformance for any operation is there to be shaped as the leader wishes and to serve as a primary source of corrective action.

The General Accounting Office examined companies that were improving their quality. Those companies used several measures to assess the impact of quality management: timeliness of delivery, reliability, order-processing time, production errors, product lead time, inventory turnover, quality cost, and cost savings. As seen in the accompanying figure, every measure improved when the company focused on quality. Reliability improved 11.5 percent. Most of the companies improved their performance in all dimensions.

Not all the companies surveyed measured the cost of quality. Those that did not cited problems of defining cost factors and the administrative burden of collecting such data. All companies that did measure it reported that these costs dropped an average of 9 percent annually. These savings included the cost of quality failures or defects (lost profits, rework, and scrap) or the cost of trying to avoid them (inspection, testing, and training).

Improvement from Focusing on Quality

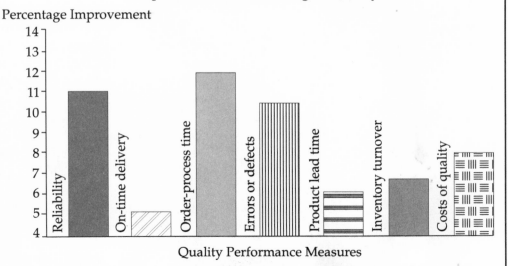

(Source: U.S. General Accounting Office)[4]

The Example of the Rejects. When I was an inspector, the manufacturing supervisor would take things I had rejected early in the month and save them. At the end of the month, when it was becoming difficult to meet schedule, he would get these back out and present them to my supervisor, who would decide that they were perfectly all right. It was a game to them.

The leader's attitude about the integrity of the system will shine through, regardless of what actions are taken or not taken. People will look to see how you "walk and talk" about it. Do your standards change as you approach the end of the reporting period?

There has been very little real progress in quality over the past dozen years, even though the quality revolution is going on. Even though the actions necessary are clearly known, they have not been implanted in the hearts of the executive corps. Yet, when you have the challenge of turning an organization around, the quickest way is through quality—through policy, education, and example.

Quality is a magic wand that pays for itself. Better than that, it is the most reliable source of profit an organization has.

REFLECTIONS

Making customers successful means creating an organization that does things right the first time. This is systems integrity. It means that everything works as planned. It is the result of a carefully constructed, yet natural, operating culture. That culture cannot be purchased or packaged. It is a reflection of the leader's personal integrity.

A "quality policy" is a direction to all employees of the organization, a promise to customers, and an agreement with suppliers. This policy says that each individual in the system will perform his or her tasks in the agreed manner.

Everyone in an organization must understand how quality is defined by the organization, what orientation produces it, what performance standard applies, and what measurement should be used.

Management's primary job is to make certain that requirements exist for every task, that the persons responsible for the job understand how to accomplish the requirements, and that the proper facilities and resources exist to accomplish the requirements. Quality is then defined as "conforming to the requirements." The performance standard is zero defects.

Identify and eliminate the costs of doing things wrong. Having the accounting department determine the price of nonconformance (error) is the best way to assure executive involvement in quality.

Customer management involves the following three aspects of relationships:

- ♦ Identifying the actual customer
- ♦ Determining the customer's needs
- ♦ Nurturing the customer

THE LEADER AND CUSTOMERS

8

The duPonts and Cornings have succeeded not primarily because of their product or research orientation but because they have been thoroughly customer-oriented also. It is constant watchfulness for opportunities to apply their technical know-how to the creation of customer-satisfying uses which accounts for their prodigious output of successful new products.

Theodore Levitt, Editor, *Harvard Business Review*

CUSTOMER MANAGEMENT

There is only one component that is absolutely required in order to have a business: a customer. Everything else can be done without, somehow or other. Those who lose sight of this pay for it. Customer management involves three aspects of relationships:

1. Identifying the actual customer,

2. Determining the customer's needs, and

3. Nurturing the customer.

IDENTIFYING THE CUSTOMER

Customers are people or organizations we do something for; in return, they give us money or some other commodity or service. Those who receive our products or services and then pay as promised are traditional customers. Customers also can be people whom we serve, even if the payment comes from somewhere else.

We have to know what success means to the customer.

Make certain you know who the customer is. This is not always obvious. For instance, college presidents do not always understand that their faculties are their primary customers. The heads of health-care operations often think that patients are their customers, but the medical professionals actually are. Think about it: no professors, no students; no students, no tuition; no doctors, no patients; no patients, no fees.

DETERMINING THE CUSTOMER'S NEEDS

We have to think of customers as people with a need that we want to fulfill. Some are easy, like a person who is hungry for a sandwich. Some customers do not know they have needs, some cannot describe their needs exactly, and some require special attention. They all want you to help them to be successful. To do that, we have to know what success means to the customer.

The Example of the Government Contractors

Early in my career, I worked with companies that made high-technology weapon systems for the government. One of the military services would ask for a weapon system, Congress would fund it, and it was ordered by a purchasing agency. The ultimate user was the customer of the purchasing agency, who would be our customer if we got the contract.

I first gained the impression that getting a customer was a function of making presentations. A whole department called "presentations" created brochures and notebooks detailing the steps we would take in order to produce what that customer wanted. Because defense procurement is such a large, complex, operation, these presentations had to impress the many people and departments involved.

Later, I began to think that money was the most important criterion, that the winner was the lowest bidder among qualified applicants. When companies like Martin, General Dynamics, Lockheed, and Boeing were competing for the same project, there was no question that each was capable of doing the job. The winner would hire many of the same people, who would be laid off from the companies that did not receive the contract.

It took me awhile to realize that the customers' real concern was not being embarrassed. The successful weapon-systems contractor was the organization that could develop a relationship with the government customer based on performance and problem avoidance.

In many cases, executives spent their time working person-to-person with the customer and letting others run the actual operation. This was not baby sitting, it was helping the customer to stay informed and involved. Many large contractors cut the customer out of the picture and developed a lack of trust. They soon gained reputations for being "arrogant" and were shunned by the military establishment.

Other Examples

Most insurance operations deal primarily with indepen-
dent and corporate agents. Several years ago, they began
to understand that these offices are their real customers,
although they advertise to the insurance buyers. They
also began to understand that insurance is pretty much
the same product regardless of the company, so the only
real differences are the relationship the user has with the
agent and the services that the corporation itself can offer.

Many manufacturing units deal with only professional customers—purchasing agents who represented
companies that need the components and products the
units produce. Others are aimed at specific customers.
One pump company organized a "little red school
house" and taught its customer's people all they needed
to know about pumps. Needless to say, it became the
standard for the business.

When I founded Philip Crosby Associates in 1979, I
started with the identification of my customer. It was
apparent to me that quality management was a real need
in U.S. business. I decided that the leaders of companies—who were paying a large amount of money for
their present quality efforts and receiving little in
return—would be my targets. If they could understand
what would work, they would do it.

I decided that our clients would learn more if they
were away from their offices, so we had them come to
Florida. We carefully set up the courses in an environment comfortable to them. The education system was
imbued with dignity. The class size was limited to twenty people. The furniture was carefully selected for com-
fort and executive ambiance. The instructors were
carefully taught; they knew the philosophy and content
of the courses and how to answer questions and conduct
evaluations.

The people who came to the classes wanted to find
out if we ran our company according to the principles of

Good market research does not have to be expensive. Customers are the best source of market research for new products and services.[1]

quality management. We did, and it took a lot of work to make it happen. The impression of participating in a zero-defect operation for a few days had a large effect on our clients. We made absolutely certain that everything worked just as it was supposed to. When something went astray, we immediately presented the class with the complete corrective action.

Nurturing the Customer

Nurturing customers does not get a great deal of attention automatically. Once the sale is complete, once the customer has moved on to the next stop, once the contact is broken, the mind switches to the new customer. There has to be a planned program of nurturing. Many companies would never need new customers if they could sell the current ones everything they need.

The Example of the Clothing Store

I worked in a men's clothing store in South Bend, Indiana while being an underpaid reliability engineer at Bendix. There I learned about nurturing. The owner of the store stood at the front door and greeted all the customers as they entered. He found out what they needed and took them to a sales person. He checked with them as they left, and he took the appropriate action if they had not been satisfied.

His brother stood back by the cash register and helped the customers to arrange credit. Each month, every customer received a message from the store, separate from the bill. Many customers received phone calls from the owners or sales persons telling them about interesting apparel that had been acquired. Each newcomer to town received a box of chocolate mints and a notice that their credit was good at the store.

Ford Motor Company figures it costs five times as much to attract a new customer as to keep a present one. Reichheld and Susser note that keeping 5% more of their customers yields a 100% increase in profits. A normal company's growth rate can be doubled by cutting by half the number of lost customers each year.[2]

The sales people were given classes continually on dealing with customers. The owners continually rearranged merchandise and displays to keep the store attractive. The result of this effort was that they had the highest sales per square foot of any men's clothing store outside Manhattan.

Then they decided to open two more stores. Soon the owners were not able to stand in their usual positions and greet customers. They asked others to take over this responsibility, but somehow no one could get worked up enough about standing in the doorway or by the cash register to make an impact on the customers like the owners had.

As they managed three stores, the brothers found themselves continually involved with details of the operations rather than with customers. Soon the incredible customer loyalty they had developed over the years began to wane. One day, the owner came to the shoe department in the main store, where I worked part time.

Nurturing customers and meeting their needs creates customer loyalty.

"Phil," he said, "I know you work here to help support your family, and we appreciate having you."

I thanked him.

"But I also notice that you apparently enjoy the work. You are always involved with something. Why is that?"

I told him that I liked people and enjoyed being able to help them find what they needed. Besides, he had a nice group of people working there.

"I used to enjoy it like that," he said, "but I guess I am just getting old. I'm tired a lot now."

To cheer him up, I thought I would ask him a few questions. "I have decided that I want to be a leader," I said. "What do you think are the most important things I need to work on?"

He smiled at me and began to perk up. "The most important part of any business is the customer," he stated firmly. "The true leader gets the priorities right and concentrates on making the customers successful."

"So what are you doing hanging around the shoe stock room?," I asked. "There aren't any customers back here."

He jumped back, startled, and stared at me. Then (and I swear this is true), he patted me on the head and walked straight to the front door. He sent the sales person at the door back into the store and went back to greeting customers.

> *The toughest thing about success is that you've got to keep on being a success.*
> —Irving Berlin

After that, he carefully selected the front door person for each store and spent a great deal of time teaching that person how to greet and help customers. He bought some time on a radio station and gave fashion hints. He spoke to groups around town and even sent me to the Rotary and PTA meetings to talk about fitting shoes.

He learned to reach out to the customers in many ways and he always made a point of listening. His brother did the same sort of things and developed a reputation for being a credit expert in the Midwest. (Bankers need clothes, too.)

STAYING IN TOUCH WITH CUSTOMERS

The single reason most executives fail to be continually effective is because they become disengaged from their customers. They either succumb to the engrossing spell of running the business or they become arrogant, or both. As a result, they begin to think that the customer is secure, that things will always be this way, and that the marketing department can take care of it all.

A Federal study found that encouraging customer complaints increased the likelihood of those customers doing business with an organization. If the company responded immediately, apologized, and guaranteed to fix it, the possibility of the customer remaining a customer rose to 95%.[3]

They then miss the changes that inevitably occur in the customers' needs. They begin to go off in a different direction from their sources of income. What I heard from the big U.S. companies when their markets began to shrink in the early 1970s was that their customers were "disloyal" and "ungrateful."

The reason this misjudgment happens over and over is that executives do not establish personal strategies for dealing with their customers. Even those who have created a business seem to gloss over this point sooner or later. The person who used to spend all day with customers now spends most of the time in a conference room. The customers are considered a commodity; it is assumed that the well-run company will always attract them. It is much like the people who love their families so much they spend all their time trying to provide for them and never get around to coming home.

The effective leader thinks about customer management with the same intensity he or she gives to finance and quality.

Customers must be identified every day; their needs must be examined and met moment by moment; and they must be nurtured so that they regard you as their preferred supplier. Your competitors would love to have your customers. At this moment, in some nation you may not know about, a few people are sitting around a table taking aim at your market.

REFLECTIONS

There is only one component that is absolutely required in order to have a business: a customer.

♦ Identifying the customer correctly is the most important step.

♦ To identify the customer's needs, you have to know what success means to the customer.

♦ The successful organization builds a relationship with the customer based on performance and avoidance of problems.

♦ There has to be a planned program of nurturing the customer.

The single reason most executives fail to be continually effective is because they become disengaged from their customers. As a result, they begin to think that the customer is secure and that the marketing department can take care of it all. They then miss the changes that inevitably occur in the customers' needs. They begin to go off in a different direction from their sources of income.

The three aspects of dealing with suppliers are selection, communication, and performance.

♦ Suppliers are selected because they have the proper product or service, they have financial integrity, and they meet our needs.

♦ Maintain constant communication with suppliers, inform them of all requirements, and assure their understanding.

♦ Continually review suppliers' performance and inform them immediately of any inadequacy or nonconformance. Expect prompt and effective corrective action when necessary.

THE LEADER AND SUPPLIERS

> *End the practice of awarding business on the basis of price tag. Instead, minimize total cost. Move toward a single supplier for any one item, on a long-term relationship of loyalty and trust.*

W. Edwards Deming

9

DEALING WITH SUPPLIERS

Everything we use in our business and personal lives comes from suppliers. The leader must take suppliers seriously and not just let some group or system select them on the basis of price. There must be policies and there must be an awareness that suppliers are like the organs of our body, providing life functions to us. They require personal attention.

- ♦ In the best restaurant I know, the chef goes down to the market every morning. His suppliers have laid out their very best for his choice. Many would be pleased to deliver directly to his place of business, but he wants to select the freshest for his customers.

- A hotel that has dealt with the same florist for twenty years has never failed to receive daily compliments from guests on the arrangements and freshness of its flowers.

- In one company, the office copier has not been out of order for three years; in another, the semiconductor components have not had to be tested in six years.

- Think about the suppliers involved with the family car: the manufacturer and its thousands of suppliers; the dealership; the bank that financed it; the place that services it; the car wash; the auto parts store; the licensing agency; the road construction companies; the traffic engineers; the road maintenance department; the radio station that gives traffic updates.

We are woven into life with our suppliers, like it or not. We need to learn to help them take good care of us. There are three aspects of dealing with suppliers:

1. Selection,
2. Communication, and
3. Performance.

All these work through relationships, just like everything else in life.

SELECTION

The store where I buy my suits is not the most expensive place I could use, nor is it the least expensive. I selected it because the people there are interested in helping their customers be the best they can. In addition to providing good materials and designs, they go another step. They place a coordinating number inside the suit jacket, the tie, and the shirt. They provide written directions for putting sports jackets and slacks together. That way I know for sure that everything is going to match. Once in a while, I decide to mix things up, but I have been learning from them all along.

As I change my clothing needs, or styles change, the store is always a step ahead of me. When we went on a cruise last year, they knew just what to provide. If I gain a few pounds, they make adjustments; when the pounds are lost, other adjustments are made. They take care of me, and I trust them. I pay their bills on time, and they respect my needs.

The traditional method of selecting suppliers, primarily in the commercial world but also in private, is to send out bids and select the least expensive option. Purchasing professionals are getting more sensitive now, but their primary concern still is price. The result of this orientation is to make the relationship one dimensional. As a result, it is negative. The same supplier rarely receives contracts in a series, so never has much understanding of or respect for the customer.

The reason for this situation is embedded in the way management has measured the performance of purchasing professionals. They were expected to concentrate on "cheap and on time." It has been that way for years. The thought of having only one source for anything was considered heresy. "The supplier would take advantage of you."

The practice of planned hostility with suppliers was never useful and now it has to be thrown away. There is no room for nonproductive effort in today's business world. We cannot afford all the checking and auditing that goes along with it.

> Someone once said, "Once is not enough," but one may be enough, at least in the area of quality. In 1980, with 5,000 suppliers and a shipment defect rate of 8%, Xerox moved to "single sourcing." (This was the forerunner of the "vendor certification" so popular in the 1990s.) As a result, Xerox's cost of materials dropped by 50% and its overhead for its material management area dropped by two-thirds. An additional bonus was the fact that defects fell from 10,000-25,000 per million to an impressive 350 per million.[1]

The best suppliers are those who recognize that their prosperity is based on the cooperation they give their customers. The best customers are those who realize that their success is based on the quality of the goods and services provided by their suppliers.

Many manufacturing companies still have 20 percent of their production areas set aside for receiving. Packages arrive continually and are scheduled for inspection or test before being sent to the stock room. The area is always full of people. There are purchasing expediters hunting for material that is needed right away; there are inspectors and testers trying to process materials; there are production-control people who want to keep their schedules. It is all unnecessary. Companies that learn how to deal with suppliers properly do not need receiving inspections in order to keep their suppliers honest.

To enter a new and practical era, it is necessary to find and develop good suppliers; to actually solicit, interview, and educate them; and to help them become successful. The best suppliers are those who recognize that their prosperity is based on the cooperation they give their customers. The best customers are those who realize that their success is based on the quality of the goods and services provided by their suppliers. Organizations need to develop a "co-prosperity" attitude to replace the money-grubbing attitude of the past.

COMMUNICATION

When we think about making suppliers successful, we have to think about more than financial return. Smart suppliers realize that your success brings them more customers. In order to ensure that they can serve you best, it is necessary to involve key suppliers in the planning activity as early as possible.

When my company first conceived a series of instructional tapes, we set up a meeting with the film producer and director, the advertising agency, the fulfillment house that fills viewer orders, the public relations firm, and the staff. Such sessions were held regularly, so the people involved communicated regularly during the process. As a result, there were no surprises during production, and everything went as planned. Each of our suppliers said that this was the first time such communication had been arranged. They then tried to encourage their other customers to do the same.

Suppliers have to understand the requirements they are expected to meet and have some opportunity to respond to those that apply to their products or services. We often do not use what we receive as well as we could because we do not know enough about the product or service to fit it into our work in the best fashion. If our suppliers feel that they are part of the team, they will help us use their products and services better.

As a project manager, I once held a suppliers conference. We took our supplier executives on a tour of our facility, so that they could see where their offerings were installed in the

> Colonel Dale A. Misner says, "Our way of turning around a contractor with such a history of long-term problems was to work with him, not against him. We help solve instead of simply identifying and then walking away, leaving the contractor to solve his own problems. We stay, in fact, until the problem is solved. We roll up our sleeves and get dirty right along with the contractor if need be. We now view ourselves as being part of the solution."

system and talk to the people involved. Several of the visitors pointed out better ways of doing things, and one even noted that we were mounting a unit upside down. (We changed our procedure, and they began putting an arrow on the unit.)

Many large companies try to control their suppliers by insisting that they comply with a preset system of management. This has proven to be worse than useless. By worse, I mean that it takes up executive time and contaminates what may be a perfectly useful way of doing things.

One contract asks the supplier to send a certificate that everything is as it is supposed to be. Can you imagine anyone including a report saying, "The contents of this package are no good"? A large manufacturing organization requires statistical-process-control charts with each order. It receives tens of thousands every year. Not one has ever indicated a process out of control. However, all these reports are kept in file cabinets so if something goes wrong, it can be shown that it wasn't the purchasing department's fault.

The most effective system specification for those who sell to you says, "Dear Supplier: We have agreed on what you are to provide and what we are to pay. When you provide it to us, we will pay you. Sincerely."

Executives who delegate policy are always in trouble, and nothing screams more for delegating than troublesome suppliers. But they are only troublesome when viewed through the policies of the past. It is necessary to make the following very clear to all involved:

1. Suppliers are to be selected because they have the proper product or service, financial integrity, and the earnest intention of meeting our needs.

2. We have the obligation to maintain constant communication with our suppliers, inform them of all requirements, and assure their understanding.

3. We will continually review our suppliers' performance and inform them immediately of any inadequacy or nonconformance, expecting prompt and effective corrective action when necessary.

PERFORMANCE

Not every company has a lot of suppliers. Some like to be vertically integrated, doing everything themselves. Some like to have others do things for them. At one time, General Motors had about 750,000 employees and 110 billion dollars in revenues; Toyota had about 90,000 employees and about 63 billion dollars in revenues. GM had twice the revenues but around eight times the

employees. The difference was in the use of suppliers.
When they are well managed, suppliers are less expensive and more manageable than a "sister" organization,
and they usually have a lower overhead.

When the goal is boosting profits by dramatically lowering costs, a business should
look first to what it buys. On average, manufacturers shell out 55 cents of each dol-
lar of revenues on goods and services, from raw materials to overnight mail. By con-
trast, labor seldom exceeds 6% of sales, overhead 3%. So purchasing exerts far
greater leverage on earnings than anything else. By shrinking the bill 5%, a typical
manufacturer adds almost 3% to net profits.

William Marx, AT&T's executive vice president for telephone products, says:
"Purchasing is by far the largest single function at AT&T. Nothing we do is more
important." Fast trackers like Daniel Carroll, AT&T's purchasing chief, have turned
to "creative collaboration." In exchange for helping key suppliers manufacture more
efficiently and thereby hold down prices, purchasers garner a share of the savings.

Companies today are packing once-fragmented purchases of services and sup-
plies into one or two companywide contracts for each. Bulk orders drive down costs.
High-volume purchasing can trim bills for services and MRO by 10% to 25%.

Cutting purchasing costs has surprisingly little to do with browbeating suppliers of raw materials and components to lower their prices. AT&T and Chrysler...see
price as just one aspect of total cost, and form enduring partnerships with suppliers
that enable them to chip away at other key costs year after year. They aim to help
suppliers shrink inventories, banish waste, and standardize components, steps that
can generate as much savings as beating down prices.

The steps to power purchasing are:

♦ *Leverage your buying power.* Find the parts and services used across groups of
plants or the entire corporation. Purchase items in large volumes from one
or two big suppliers instead of a patchwork of vendors.

♦ *Commit to a handful of suppliers on which you can depend.* Invite the leading
suppliers to compete for your business. Choose two or three that offer the
best combination of price and productivity improvements.

♦ *Work together to reduce total cost.* Dispatch your production people to help
suppliers lower inventories and cut waste. Benchmark your suppliers'
prices, costs, and technology against those of their rivals at least once a year.
If your vendors have slipped, help them to regain their edge.

Says Jack Barry, a purchasing specialist with EDS's management consulting division:
"As we move to a seller's market, companies win by treating suppliers not as adver-
saries but partners."[2]

The result produced by suppliers has to be exactly as agreed. Exactly, not close to it. You do not want to have to store things because suppliers are not reliable. You have to be very firm about this. Ten years ago, most of my manufacturing clients had inventory systems that required separate buildings and complex control systems. Today those buildings are empty or are used for something more profitable. This has been achieved by getting suppliers interested in quality.

The way to measure the effectiveness of suppliers is in relation to price, schedule, and quality. Do not get involved with a sliding scale. The price is either appropriate or not; the deliveries are either on time or not; the requirements are either met completely or not.

THE SUPPLIER-ORIENTATION MEETING

Suppliers should be invited to attend orientation meetings at least once a year. Only senior people should be asked to represent suppliers (sales people will agree to and promise anything). A well-run, one-day conference is best. The goals are to make certain that your suppliers know your policies and that they will be met; to introduce them to your people and your way of working; and to build better relationships.

Start the meeting precisely on time. State what it is all about, briefly emphasizing the importance of an ongoing relationship based on world-class performance. Emphasize the competition that exists

© *Walter Hodges/Tony Stone Images*

A supplier-orientation meeting should be held at least once a year.

and that working together is the way to overcome it. State that open communication is the way to work together—both formal and informal communication.

Invite a well-known, outside speaker to comment on the world situation for business, with special attention to your industry or specialty. Ask some suppliers to prepare remarks about their needs, and have your purchasing managers discuss their concerns. After the speeches, give everyone the chance to participate in an open discussion augmented by written questions. (Some people feel better handing in a question than standing up and speaking.)

Close the meeting by reintroducing the purchasing people and other personnel the suppliers should contact. Give the suppliers a package of information on your organization and on any special project with which they will be involved. Follow up with a letter.

In dealing with suppliers, have no tolerance for those who miss schedules, costs, or quality. Make certain that those who work well with you make an appropriate return on their investment and, when possible, give them long-range commitments. (That way, they can upgrade their facilities and train their people better.)

EDUCATING OTHERS

Purchasing is one of those areas that senior management does not think about unless something is going wrong. It is a great area in which to build a reputation in an organization, but it requires educating everyone involved.

To obtain the proper attention, begin by figuring how much it costs to start with a new supplier. It is basically the same as employee turnover. The money saved by getting a lower bid is spent quickly. It is much better to encourage existing suppliers to manage their processes to produce lower costs. (Another hidden expense is storing materials. Henry Ford's idea of "just in time" inventory eliminates that. Materials are brought in when they are needed.)

Remind your suppliers of how many people and processes are affected if they do not do exactly what is promised. Then reward them for doing exactly what is promised. Remember that educating suppliers is only half the task; the other half is educating people in your company to regard and deal with suppliers as partners.

REFLECTIONS

The relationships with suppliers are some of the most important relationships an organization has. The three main aspects of these relationships are selection, communication, and performance.

Carefully selecting suppliers who have the proper product or service and financial integrity, and maintaining open and timely communication on standards, obviates the need for inspection.

Because the quality of our products depends on the quality of the materials we receive from our suppliers, we need to work with our suppliers to ensure that they are able to do for us what we need them to do. Suppliers have to understand the requirements they are expected to meet and have some opportunity to respond to those that apply to their products or services. Suppliers also can help us to use their products and services better.

In return, we need to let our suppliers know that they can rely on us for advice, assistance, and business, as long as they maintain their standards.

The way to measure the effectiveness of suppliers is in relation to price, schedule, and quality. The price is either appropriate or not; the deliveries are either on time or not; the requirements are either met or not.

The goals of the annual supplier-orientation meeting are to make certain that our suppliers know our policies; to introduce them to our people and our ways of working; and to build better relationships with them.

A leader needs to be concerned with three aspects of employee relations: selection, education, and climate.

The four things that produce a positive work climate are:

- ◆ Access to management
- ◆ A realistic support system
- ◆ A fair evaluation system
- ◆ Adequate compensation

THE LEADER AND EMPLOYEES

> *Today's leader is a person who can communicate and motivate.*
>
> Stuart R. Levine, CEO
> Dale Carnegie & Associates

10

RELATIONSHIPS

Very few parts of an organization are recognized as being able to do their work right the first time, cheerfully and efficiently. There is no better way to identify yourself as a leader than to accomplish this in your area of responsibility. It is not difficult; all that is necessary is to have your employees on your side.

Employees at any level in any organization in any part of the world will work just as hard as they want to and be as dedicated and effective as they desire. The task of the leader is to help them want to give the organization their all. This cannot be accomplished through bribes or threats; it must be done through relationships.

Relationships are based on the leader's deliberately creating a climate of consideration and achievement that people recognize as genuine. When managers do not relate to employees, they create antagonism. Some leaders think it is easier to manage when you do not have to be concerned about people's feelings or well being. However, when people sense a lack of interest in them, they respond in kind.

Two things happen in an organization when relationships do not exist between leaders and employees:

♦ It takes a lot more people to do the work, because people will not take responsibility for results beyond their immediate tasks;

♦ It is difficult to achieve improvement, because employees feel little loyalty to the organization.

To prevent or eliminate such problems, and to provide a positive environment, a leader needs to be concerned with three things:

1. Selection,

2. Education, and

3. Climate.

The best leader is the one who has sense enough to pick good men to do what he wants done, and the self-restraint to keep from meddling with them while they do it.

—Theodore Roosevelt

SELECTION

Every project begins with the selection of the raw materials. At that moment, the future of the operation is determined, to a great degree.

Selecting those who work for you is important. Not everyone has the same capacity to help you to become successful. The wise leader eliminates people who are not capable of producing the desired results, despite efforts to "develop" them. Not everyone will agree with what you want to do. The wise leader also eliminates those who openly disagree with the leader's vision and those on whom consideration and appreciation are wasted.

My experience in large corporations is that some employees in each area are counterproductive. They are more trouble than asset. Few of them can be turned around through frank discussions and reassurance. They became set in their attitudes early in life and see no reason to change.

People who are simply anti-management often will disagree and sabotage efforts simply for the sake of doing so. Such people often do not recognize when they are being treated well. Other employees may be simply too negative or too difficult for others to get along with. It is not possible to build a successful organization with such raw material. Problem employees take up too much management time and sow the seeds of discontent.

Identify those who are good at their jobs and enthusiastic about their work. You can fertilize and nourish them. Let the others go as gently as possible.

Your goal is to hire enthusiastic people and then not make them unenthusiastic.

It is also important for the leader to have a hand in the selection process, not to just rely on the personnel department. Employee selection usually focuses on the work skills involved and the applicant's experience in doing the job. Educational background is checked out, and often performance tests are administered. Very little usually is known about a potential employee's attitudes.

The leader of the functional area should interview applicants after they have passed the first layer of checking for technical and educational competence. The leader should concentrate on identifying the person's attitudes about life and business, not on explaining how the organization works.

It is a good idea to ask if the person has any questions about the organization, the job, or anything else. Then be quiet, to give the person a chance to think and respond. If the person has no questions, you may assume that the person has little interest in the organization and is just looking for a paycheck. If the person asks about benefits, it is possible to determine his or her concerns right away. The objective is to find someone who is interested in the work of the organization and looking for a place where he or she can obtain job satisfaction and an opportunity for growth.

Positive people attract positive people. Identify a few existing employees who are positive and let them help to interview applicants. After all, they are the ones who are going to have to work with them. I encouraged my employees to recommend their friends and family members for employment. When employees are part of bringing people in, they tend to help one another stay enthusiastic and productive. Your goal is to hire enthusiastic people and then not make them unenthusiastic.

EDUCATION

Once people are selected, they need to be placed immediately into the education stream. This begins with a good orientation program, which most organizations do not have. I do not mean a one-hour orientation. Even if an employee comes from another part of the same organization, you need to provide a thoughtful orientation. People are never quite so attentive later as they are in their first few days in a new job.

New employees need to understand the vision, policies, and work ethic of the organization; they need to meet their coworkers and learn who does what. They need to have their jobs explained by their manager, not by the person at the next desk.

There are two forms of education: that which the organization provides and that which the employees do for themselves. Organizations should do everything possible to develop the habit of continual education in employees. The company should pay for any courses employee want to take—even basket weaving. In this day of rapidly changing everything, nothing is not applicable. The intent is to get people into the habit of learning.

Often "management development" programs don't work because the wrong people are selected and they are taught the wrong things. Don't waste time trying to develop people; help them to develop themselves.

The organization should provide education in communication and other interpersonal work skills as well as in technical skills. Quality-improvement concepts must be taught, and job-skills training should be part of every job change. Employees should meet in an open forum at least once a month to be kept up to date on organizational developments and to build relationships. This also generates communication and mutual respect.

Conducting regular all-personnel meetings is one way of keeping employees involved with the organization. The leader should avoid being out of town when these meetings are scheduled to be held. The leader should talk about operations, and the financial officer should talk about the company's growth and revenues. The human resources person can introduce new people and announce any promotions or job changes. Committees and projects can be reported on by those involved. Everyone can be given the opportunity to say something or ask questions. Rumors can be addressed and clarified. This gives all employees a chance to see one another and build better relationships.

An organizational newsletter (either printed or distributed by electronic mail) can contain announcements of company events, major contracts or

> Motorola founder Paul Galvin's belief that a company is only as effective as the people who staff it guides how the Motorola workforce is selected, trained, and motivated to succeed. In 1992, for example, Motorola spent approximately $100 million on employee training. With a liberal offsite education and tuition-reimbursement program, the company believes it doubles that figure annually to help its employees better themselves. A Motorola quarterly report showed record sales in January to March, 1995, with earnings of $6 billion, up 28% from the same time period in 1994.[1]

sales, schedules, want ads, and anything else in which employees might be interested. People appreciate the consistency with which they receive information and attention from such vehicles.

CLIMATE

These builders [of the great early American corporations like IBM, Procter & Gamble, and Johnson & Johnson] saw their role as creating an environment—in effect a culture—in their companies in which employees could be secure and thereby do the work necessary to make the business a success.[2]

To create a climate of consideration in which people are motivated to do their best, we can begin by asking ourselves, "What would we like to have in terms of a work climate?" and "How would we like to be treated?"

Every organization has to be viewed regularly as a "clean sheet of paper." If jobs and systems have lives of their own, the operation will become congested with privilege and clogged with tradition. It will grow in people but not in effectiveness. When it becomes too unwieldy, unplanned reductions will have to occur. Organizations that stay tight and effective do not suffer that fate.

We do not want to offer jobs guaranteed for life, but we do want employees to know that those who produce and grow will be treated properly. Establishing a policy of how people are treated in an organization begins with determining the purpose of the organization. "To earn a profit" is not a well-thought-out answer. The purpose of a company has to be to help people have productive lives. These people include customers and suppliers as well as employees. In addition to compensation and benefit programs, the company provides an identity that gives meaning to people's lives.

Four things contribute to creating a climate that produces creativity, productivity, and a pleasant place to work. These four things are as follows.

ACCESS TO MANAGEMENT

Access to management doesn't mean the manager's door is always open; it means that any employee can communicate with management, offer suggestions, and feel heard and considered an important part of the organization. It is your job to make it known that such communication is welcomed. Periodically talking to employees at all levels can help to keep you aware of what is going on in the organization.

Y ou don't hear things that are bad about your company unless you ask. It is easy to hear good tidings, but you have to scratch to get the bad news.

—Thomas J. Watson, Jr.

Management has to go where the employees are in order to accomplish this. When I decided to leave one company, the president found out about it and asked me why I had been unhappy. I told him that my ideas were scoffed at while the operation slowly deteriorated. "You should have told me," he said. "The only time I see you is at the annual picnic," I replied.

A REALISTIC SUPPORT SYSTEM

Employee benefits should include a prevention-oriented health care system, a funded pension program, child care assistance, and private counseling when needed. A properly selected and managed benefit program costs around 35 percent of compensation. However, it will increase productivity because it will take people's minds off other concerns. For instance, parents may spend a great part of the afternoon on the telephone checking up on their children who are home from school. With child care assistance—which costs very little—that distraction is eliminated, and the parents are grateful.

A FAIR EVALUATION SYSTEM

The most dismal part of management is trying to evaluate employees. Since individual criterion differ, it is almost impossible to evaluate employees equitably. It is much better to ask employees for their goals, for six months and twelve months. Then discuss the steps

The amount a person uses his imagination is inversely proportional to the amount of punishment he will receive for using it.

—Roger Von Oech, in
A Whack on the Side of the Head

necessary to accomplish the goals and agree on how to measure the results over time. All the leader has to do is to help employees keep their goals high and challenging, yet measurable and realistic.

ADEQUATE COMPENSATION

Money is not a great motivator, but lack of money is a great demotivator. When I was younger, I often changed jobs and companies because I did not make enough. As I learned and became more valuable, the companies had no way of adjusting to my progress. In each case, the person hired to replace me was paid more than I had been.

In the past, management in many organizations was locked into a seniority concept: compensation and responsibility were based on age and time at work. There is a great deal more awareness today that employees make the company instead of the other way around. "Knowledge workers" are the key to success in the global economy. They have to be raised in a climate of consideration that makes them proud to work there.

This can be accomplished, in part, by selecting employees carefully, educating them continually, and creating a climate that breeds success for the employees, the organization, and its customers and suppliers.

REFLECTIONS

The first task in creating good employee relations is the selection of employees.

Employee education begins with a good orientation program. New employees need to understand the vision and policies of the organization; meet their coworkers and learn who does what; and have their jobs explained by their manager, not by the person at the next desk.

Organizations should do everything possible to develop the habit of continual education in employees, including providing educational reimbursement. The organization also should provide education in interpersonal skills and teamwork as well as in technical skills.

It is important to keep employees up to date on organizational developments. The truth is almost always preferable to the gleanings of the rumor mill.

Four things contribute to creating a positive organizational climate:

♦ Access to Management: Any employee should feel free to offer suggestions.

♦ A Realistic Support System: Effective employee benefits increase productivity because they take people's minds off other concerns.

♦ A Fair Evaluation System: The appraisal system should include a planning session in which the employee participates with the manager in setting the employee's goals and deciding how progress will be measured.

♦ Adequate Compensation: Workers should receive a level of compensation that reflects their contribution to the organization. This does not always mean that managers and executives should be paid more than other employees.

The boss-employee relationship is managed through:

- ♦ Agreement
- ♦ Help
- ♦ Prevention

THE LEADER AND BOSSES

> *Men in great places are thrice servants: servants of the sovereign or state, servants of fame, and servants of business.*
>
> Francis Bacon, 1561-1626

11

RELATIONSHIPS WITH BOSSES

The title of this chapter refers to "bosses" because even if we are leaders ourselves, we have to be concerned with many people who have the ability to affect our professional lives for good or ill.

In modern business, there is someone over almost everyone, whether it be a board of directors, a legislature, financial backers, or others. We usually do not select these people ourselves, unless we have approached them for participation or employment. We may or may not like and respect them. Because of numerous variables that can change at any moment, we need to be able to handle these arrangements and turn them into something positive for everyone involved.

Relationships with bosses require a different focus than do relationships with customers, suppliers, and employees. With the latter, we are able to supply the movement and energy; with bosses we are engaged in a great deal of defensive work.

The key is managing the boss-employee relationship. There are three aspects of this:

- ♦ Agreement
- ♦ Help
- ♦ Prevention

AGREEMENT

The most successful managers are those that can quickly grasp how their bosses think.

—Amy Bermar

The bosses who liked me provided practical advice and helped advance my career. I learned very quickly not to hop on my white horse and charge into the organization, but to take a little time to make sure that I understood an assignment in the way that my boss intended. This was an extremely valuable learning.

I asked the following types of questions:

- ♦ What result is expected?
- ♦ How soon is it anticipated?
- ♦ How will I know when I'm through?
- ♦ Are there any ground rules I don't know about (e.g., don't leave town; don't spend any money)?
- ♦ Is there anyone I should not involve?

The same sorts of questions apply in a regular job. Never let a supervisor, of any level, make up his or her own criteria for measuring your performance. Always supply it in one way or another and get specific agreement.

A leader has to have an awareness of what is going on. Awareness means knowing what the job is meant to accomplish and how results will be measured. This means, for example, that if you are in charge of customer service, you know how much time your bosses think should elapse between a customer complaint and a satisfactory answer; what the turnaround time is now; how much time you have to improve the operation; what sort of status report is desired; and to whom you should report.

These things need to be worked out as part of daily communication, and you should record everything. When the boss's peer group meets to select the next executive, you want to have input based on hard facts. Lacking them, you may be judged on the basis of how they feel about you that week.

A CEO was surprised when his board of directors asked for his resignation after only eighteen months. The board was interested in one set of goals, and he was doing a great job with a different, completely opposite, set of goals. If he had been a poor achiever, he would still be there. He was unaware of the board's wishes, and he paid the price.

One can get so involved with solving a problem or producing a product that one forgets to include others who should be included or to be courteous to others. That is always a mistake. People who are excluded or offended become your enemies rather than your allies. It is important to know who should be included, consulted, or thanked before you begin a project.

HELP

Senior managers are continually looking for people who will help them to be successful. They will reward and promote such people. Helping the boss to be successful does not mean groveling or being a "yes person."

It is important to find out what the boss wants and do it right away. If you respond to the boss this way, much of your time can be spent doing what you really want to do.

A.T. Kearney's research on successful and run-of-the-mill Fortune 500 companies discovered that CEOs of top-performing companies had one unique characteristic. All but one had been appointed from inside the company and had been the CEO for more than sixteen years.[1]

Sometimes it is helpful to categorize a boss in order to know what type of help to provide. There are three types of bosses: arrogant, consistent, and indecisive.

1. Arrogant. Serve an arrogant boss as best you can while quietly searching for a way out. It will never be possible to make an arrogant boss look good enough to satisfy his or her self-image. Arrogant bosses also change their minds frequently, and that includes their opinions of you.

Do not confuse confidence with arrogance. There are a few people who are overwhelmingly competent, so if they talk about something they did, it most likely is true. If you have the chance to work for or with someone like that, grab it. However, do not let yourself be consumed in the other person's flame. Learn what you can, and then move on.

2. Consistent. There are thoughtful executives who establish clear visions, lay out plans, guide subordinates purposefully, and accomplish their goals. They are candid, courteous, and respected. If you are not doing well, they will tell you in a way that will help. They are almost impossible to fool and have empathy with employees and the company. You can trust them.

Consistent bosses expect you to perform the agreed actions exactly as promised. Anything less will produce distrust about the next time, if there is one.

*S*ome people, however long their experience or strong their intellect, are temperamentally incapable of reaching firm decisions.
—James Callaghan, former English Prime Minister

3. Indecisive. There are people who do not like to make decisions or take a stand. Often they have very little vision. It really is not possible to help make them successful. However, it is possible to be observed helping them to avoid being unsuccessful.

Some people have become masters at this. They schedule the boss, write the speeches, meet with people, introduce people, read the mail, run programs, and receive little thanks. But others know what is going on, and reward comes eventually.

PREVENTION

Prevention is a specific responsibility of the executive. Keeping unfortunate things from happening is a result of being able to look at programs and processes that are being implemented and foresee the results.

Just as important as not making financial mistakes or not sending a customer something that is not as promised is making sure that you do not self-destruct. Certain actions are sure to land you in the leadership black hole. The following are some of those things.

Embarrassing the boss. I remember a meeting filled with important people in which one of my colleagues questioned an expenditure. He emphatically stated that the expense had not been well thought out and was a waste of money. The person under attack shrugged and suggested that the questioner ask his own boss (who was sitting next to him) about the expenditure, since that was where it had originated. Smiling through gritted teeth, the boss indicated that the subject would be discussed at a later meeting.

Another way to embarrass the boss is to fail to perform a task that the organization has committed to do.

Socializing with the boss. It is essential to have friendly relationships with one's bosses, but it is a bad idea to become "buddies" with them. This may be particularly true if a boss is of the opposite sex. There are too many things that can be misconstrued. It is important to remain professional yet concerned for the welfare and prosperity of one's bosses.

It is never a good idea to establish an after-work relationship with a boss. It is all right to play golf on

In every enterprise consider where you would come out.

—Publilius Syrus,
c. 42 B.C.

occasion as part of business; it is all right to eat and drink together while traveling. Eating lunch together once in a while on a scheduled basis during work is fine. It is good to be close enough personally to be able to speak clearly about any business subject and make strategy together. But it is not smart to engage in social activities with the boss. You will always be the subordinate, even when you are president and the boss is chairperson. You will be doing what the boss wants to do and/or running errands of some kind. That lowers the respect others have for you.

Misunderstandings. It is important to prevent misunderstandings. Whether an organization is large or small, the right people need to have the right information at the right time. That is what separates the marvelous leaders from the ordinary ones: a communication system that everyone understands, in which necessary information is timely and well identified, analysis is well planned and well executed, data are distributed in the quickest and most efficient manner, and everyone has access to real-time information that is appropriate to their jobs. There are no spiders spinning useless webs.

The importance of bosses in a leader's life cannot be overstated. That is how you learn the inner workings of the organization and where the keys are turned that give you the opportunities that shape your career. The influence of bosses is stronger than that of anyone else, for better or worse. With consideration and innovation, you can make these relationships that will advance your career dramatically.

REFLECTIONS

Almost every leader in modern business reports to—or is responsible to—someone, whether it be financial backers or a board of directors.

It is important to ascertain what the boss actually wants accomplished and when it is to be done. It also is important to find out if there are any other considerations (or people) that need to be taken into account.

Awareness means knowing what the job is meant to accomplish and how the results will be measured.

It is not possible to make an arrogant boss look good enough to satisfy his or her self-image.

Consistent bosses think out the entire process and will expect you to perform the agreed actions exactly as promised and on time.

Indecisive bosses can learn to rely on you to make them look good.

Prevention includes not embarrassing the boss; not socializing with the boss; and working to prevent misunderstandings.

Everyone should have access to real-time information that is appropriate to their jobs. There needs to be a communication system that everyone understands, with information that is timely and necessary, with well-planned and well-done analysis, and with data distributed in the most efficient manner.

Notes

INTRODUCTION

1. Bruskin Goldring Research survey for Tompkins Associates, 1995.

CHAPTER 1

1. Walter Kiechel III, "How To Spot an Empty Suit," *Fortune*, November 20, 1989, 227-229.

2. Ibid.

3. H.C. Bunke, "Pax Americana," *Business Horizons*, January-February 1990, 3-8.

4. Mark Stahlman, "Creative Destruction at IBM," *The Wall Street Journal*, January 6, 1993, A10.

CHAPTER 2

1. *The Toastmaster*, P.O. Box 9052, Mission Viejo, CA 92690.

2. Bruce Farr, "Motorola's Renewable Leadership," *Future* (University of Phoenix), Fall 1995, 8-11.

CHAPTER 3

1. Philip B. Crosby, *Leading: The Art of Becoming an Executive* (New York: McGraw-Hill, 1990), 8.

2. Darell Huff, *How to Lie with Statistics* (New York: W.W. Norton, 1954).

3. Stephen Potter, *Some Notes on Lifemanship: With a Summary of Recent Researches in Gamesmanship* (New York: Henry Holt, 1950).

4. C. Northcote Parkinson, *Parkinson's Law* (Boston: Houghton Mifflin, 1957).

5. Clarence B. Randall, *The Folklore of Management* (Boston: Little, Brown, 1961).

6. Henry Ford and Samuel Crowther, *My Life and Work* (Big Business; Economic Power in a Free Society Series), Reproduction of 1922 ed. (Salem, NH: Ayer).

7. Will Durant and Ariel Durant, *The Story of Civilization* (10 vols.) (New York: Simon & Schuster, 1935-1967).

8. Will Durant, *The Story of Philosophy: The Lives and Opinions of the Great Philosophers* (New York: Simon & Schuster, 1967).

9. Keith H. Hammonds, "Where Did They Go Wrong?" *The Quality Imperative* (published by Business Week), October 25, 1991, 38.

10. *The Toastmaster*, op. cit.

11. Roger Von Oech, *A Whack on the Side of the Head* (New York: Warner, 1983).

12. Blake Ives and Richard O. Mason, "Can Information Technology Revitalize Your Customer Service?" *The Academy of Management Executive*, vol. 4, no. 4, November 1990, 57-63.

13. Bob Laird, "USA Snapshots," *USA Today*. Source:

Sibson & Co., Association for Manufacturing Excellence.

CHAPTER 5

1. U.S. Department of Commerce. "Export Programs and Services" (pamphlet) (Washington, DC: Author), 2.

2. James McCartney, "Buy American Only a Sellout to Politics," *Washington State Journal,* February 2, 1992, 1C.

CHAPTER 6

1. National Association for the Self-Employed. *The Small Business Resource Guide* (Business Administration pamphlet) (Harst, TX: Author), 4.

CHAPTER 7

1. Craig R. Hickman and Michael A. Silva, *Creating Excellence* (New American Library, 1984).

2. Michael O'Neil, "Beyond May I Help You," *The Quality Imperative* (published by Business Week), October 25, 1991, 100.

3. Allan I. Mendelowitz, "Comprehensive Quality Management" (General Accounting Office statement to the U.S. House of Representatives Subcommittee in Science, Space and Technology), (GAO/T-NSIAD-90-22), March 20, 1990, 6-7, 76-77.

4. U.S. General Accounting Office, *Management Practices: U.S. Companies Improve Performance Through Quality Efforts* (Washington, DC: Author, May 2, 1991), 19-35.

CHAPTER 8

1. Susan Grego and Michael P. Cronin, "On-the-Cheap Market Research," *Inc.,* vol. 14, no. 6, June 1992, 108.

2. Frank Rose, "Now Quality Means Service Too," *Fortune,* April 22, 1991, 100.

3. Technical Assistance Research Programs (TARP) Institute. *Consumer Complaint Handling in America: Summary of Findings and Recommendations* (Washington, DC: White House Office of Consumer Affairs).

CHAPTER 9

1. "The Benefits of Single-Supplier Relationships," *Managing Technology Today,* vol. 1, no. 1, May 1992, 5.

2. Shawn Tully, "Purchasing's New Muscle," *Fortune,* vol. 131, no. 3, February 20, 1995, 75-83.

CHAPTER 10

1. Bruce Farr, "Motorola's Renewable Leadership," *Future* (University of Phoenix), Fall 1995, 8-11.

2. Terrence E. Deal and Allan A. Kennedy, *Corporate Cultures* (New York: Addison-Wesley, 1982).

CHAPTER 11

1. Fred G. Steingraber, "Managing in the 1990's," *Business Horizons,* vol. 33, no. 1, January-February 1990, 63.

Index

A

Absolutes of leadership, 2, 3-4
"Accomplisher" leadership style, 23-24, 25, 27-33
Actions, people-driven, 2, 3
Adaptability, importance of, 21-22
Agenda. *See* Leadership agenda
Agreements, boss-employee, 118-119
Ally, Carl, 42
American Quality Foundation, 40
Analysis, decision making and, 15
Anti-management attitudes, 109
Apollo 13 flight, 13
Aristotle, 38-39
Atmosphere, establishing, 41
Augustine, Norman R., 69
Awards programs, 43-45

B

Bankruptcy, preventing, 67
Barry, Jack, 101
Barton, Clara, 4
Bermar, Amy, 118
Boettinger, Henry M., 27
Bonaparte, Napoleon, 45
Books, learning from, 36-39
Boss-employee relations, 117-122
Bosses, types of, 120-121
Budgeting. *See* Financial-measurement systems
Business beliefs, conventional, 37
Business culture, 63
Business loans, 57
Business magazines, 39-40
Business needs, changes in, 64-66
Business startups, 62, 71

C

Cadbury, Adrian, 45
Callaghan, James, 120
"Caretaker" leadership style, 18-22, 25
Cash flow, using, 66-68
Causation, as a leadership activity, 6
CEOs, characteristics of, 119
Change, importance of, 7, 21-22, 64-66
Choice, as a leadership activity, 5
Churchill, Winston, 29
Clients, learning from, 42
Cohen, Allan, 16
Communication, 98-100, 112-113

Communication systems, 122, 123
Consistency, in decision making, 45
"Contract with America," 23
"Co-prosperity" attitude, 98
Corporate climate, 107-108, 112-114, 115
Corporate culture, 74
"Creative collaboration," 101
Creativity, as a leadership activity, 5
Crosby, Philip, ix-x. *See also* Philip Crosby Associates
Customer management, 84-93
Customers
    determining the needs of, 86-89
    identifying, 86, 88
    nurturing, 89-92
    staying in touch with, 91-92
Customer service, 73-74

D

Debt, 63
Decision making, 15, 45-46, 47
Deliberate action, 2-3
Deming, W. Edwards, 73, 95
"Destructor" leadership style, 9-12, 25
Documentation, of current conditions, 73
Drucker, Peter, 29
Durant, Will, 38

E

Education
    of employees, 110-112,.115
    for purchasing, 103-104
    for quality, 77-78
Emerson, Ralph Waldo, 50
Employee-boss relations, 117-122
Employees
    benefits for, 113, 115
    compensating, 114, 115
    educating, 110-112, 115
    evaluating, 113-114, 115
    relations with, 107-115
    respect for, 41
    selecting, 108-110
"Empty suit" management, 16
Expenses, unplanned, 65-66

F

Failing companies, turning around, 62-63
Farsightedness, 7

Financial analysis, 69
Financial leadership, 61-63
Financial-measurement systems, 68-70, 71
Financial problems, preventing, 66-68
Folklore of Management, The (Randall), 37
Ford, Henry, 37
Ford Motor Company, 89
Frankfurter, Felix, 51

G

Galvin, Paul, 111
Gandhi, Mohandas, 4
Geneen, Harold, 6, 35, 41, 62
General Motors Corporation, 100-101
Global economy, 56, 59
Goals
    employee, 113-114
    long-range, 27-28
    measurable, 31
    stating, 33
Grove, Andrew S., 49

H

Halpin, Jim, 41
How to Live with Statistics (Huff), 35-36
Huff, Darell, 35-36
Huxley, Aldous, 42

I

Incentive programs, 44
Innovation, 42-45, 47
International Business Machines (IBM), 20, 21
International market, 56
ITT Corporation, 31-32, 40

J

"Just-in-time" inventory, 37, 103-104

K

Kirkland, Lane, 63
"Knowledge workers," 114
Korn, Lester, 55

L

Leaders
    actions taken by, 5-6
    developing, 4-7
    motivations of, 28
    personal characteristics of, xii

Leadership. *See also* Absolutes of leadership
  action and, 2, 3
  defined, 1-7
  integrity of, 74
Leadership agenda, 3, 27-33
  organizational, 29-33
  personal, 27-28
  presenting, 30-31
  slogans for, 33
  stating, 31-32
Leadership personalities, 8, 9-25
Leadership-Personality Grid, 24
Leadership styles, 9-24. *See also* Personality types
Leadership talent,
  self-examination for, 6-7
Learning, 47
  from books, 36-39
  from clients, 42
  importance of, 35-36
  from mentors, 41
  from newspapers and magazines, 39-40
  from workers, 40-41
Levine, Stuart R., 107
Levinson, Harry, 18
Levitt, Thomas, 85
Luce, Henry R., 7

M
Magazines, learning from, 39-40
Management. *See also* Quality management
  access to, 112-113, 115
  ineffective, 16, 74
  open system of, 41
  respect for, 41
  support for, 119-121
Management-development programs, 111
Market research, 88
McGowan, William C., 67
Mentors, learning from, 41
Mill, John Stuart, 61
Misner, Dale A., 99
Misunderstandings, preventing, 122
Money, 63-66. *See also* Financial-measurement systems
Motivation, of leaders, 28
Motorola Corporation, 32, 111
My Life and Work (Ford), 37

N
Newsletters, organizational, 111-112
Newspapers, learning from, 39-40
Nonconformance, price of, 81, 83

O
Open-management systems, 41
Operating culture, 75, 83
Operating philosophy, 34, 47
Organizational agenda, 26, 29-33

P
Patience, as a leadership characteristic, 7
Performance standards, 80
Personal agenda, 26
Personality types. *See also* Leadership-Personality Grid
  accomplisher, 23-24
  caretaker, 18-22
  destructor, 9-12
  preparer, 22-23
  procrastinator, 12-18
Personal philosophy, 35-46
Personnel meetings, 111
Persuasion, as a leadership activity, 6
Philip Crosby Associates, 28, 42, 88
Philosophy. *See also* Operating philosophy
  creating, 35
  personal, 35-46
Planning, 3, 32
Potter, Stephen, 36
"Preparer" leadership style, 22-23, 25
Prevention, importance of, 79-80, 121-122
Priorities, financial, 71
"Procrastinator" leadership style, 12-18, 25
Purchasing function, 101, 103-104

Q
Quality, 73-82
  defining, 83
  ensuring, 76-82
  measuring, 80-82
Quality management, 7
  absolutes of, 72, 78-82
  impact of, 81
Quality movement, 2
"Quality policy," 76-77, 83

R
Randall, Clarence B., 37
Relationships, organizational, 49-53
Requirements, conformance to, 78, 83
Respect, importance of, 49
Results, orientation toward, 43, 46

Revenue-producing areas, isolating, 32, 33
Roosevelt, Eleanor, 39
Roosevelt, Theodore, 108
Rousseau, Jean Jacques, 39

S
"Single sourcing," 97
Small Business Administration, 61
Story of Philosophy (Durant), 38
Supplier-orientation meetings, 102-103, 105
Suppliers, 95-104
  communicating with, 98-100
  dealing with, 95-96
  performance of, 100-103
  selecting, 96-98, 105
Swiggett, Jim, 9
Systems, understanding, 42
Systems integrity, 75-82, 83

T
Talent, recognizing, 22
Technological advances, 59
Travel, effective, 56-58, 59

V
Vendor certification, 97
Vision, promoting, 31
Voltaire, 39
Von Oech, Roger, 114

W
Watson, Thomas J., Jr., 113
Welch, John, 64
Willey, Tom, 41
Work, leadership as, 3
Work climate, positive, 106
Workers. *See also* Employees
  learning from, 40-41
  rewarding, 43-45
Worldliness, 55-58

X-Z
Xerox Corporation, 97
"Zero defects" concept, 80

THE WARREN BENNIS EXECUTIVE BRIEFING SERIES

*"To survive in the 21st century, we're going to need
a new generation of leaders, not managers.
This series is an exciting collection of business books
written to help your leaders meet the challenges of the new millennium."*

Dr. Warren Bennis
USC Professor and Founding Chairman, The Leadership Institute
Author, *On Becoming a Leader* and *An Invented Life*

Tailored to the needs of busy professionals and authored by subject matter experts, the *Warren Bennis Executive Briefing Series* helps leaders acquire significant knowledge in the face of information overload. All *Series* titles utilize the SuperReading comprehension/retention editing and design techniques made famous by Howard Berg, *The Guinness Book of World Records'* "World's Fastest Reader." Read these 128-page books in just two hours!

TITLES INCLUDE:

Fabled Service: Ordinary Acts, Extraordinary Outcomes	Betsy Sanders
The 21st Century Organization: *Reinventing Through Reengineering*	Warren Bennis/ Michael Mische
Managing Globalization in the Age of Interdependence	George Lodge
Coach to Coach: Business Lessons from the Locker Room	John Robinson
The Faster Learning Organization: *Gain and Sustain the Competitive Edge*	Bob Guns
The Absolutes of Leadership	Philip Crosby
Customer Inspired Quality: *Looking Backward Through the Telescope*	James Shaw
INFORelief: Stay Afloat in the InfoFlood	Maureen Malanchuk

Contact your local bookstore for all *Warren Bennis Executive Briefing Series* titles, or order directly from Pfeiffer & Company Customer Service, **1-800-274-4434**, 2780 Circleport Drive, Erlanger, KY, 41018. For special sales or bulk purchases, call Pfeiffer & Company Group Sales at 1-800-320-2270.

About the Author

Philip B. Crosby has been a quality-management professional; senior executive of a large, international corporation; founder and CEO of a major training and consulting corporation; author of ten books that have sold millions of copies; and well-known lecturer on the subjects of quality, management, and leadership. He currently is chairman of Career IV, Inc.

After service with the U.S. Navy, Mr. Crosby worked as a reliability engineer with Bendix Corporation and then as a quality manager with Martin. Finding the concept of inevitable error too costly, he developed the concept of "zero defects" in 1961. In 1965, he became corporate quality director at ITT; in 1968, he became a vice president of ITT, responsible for quality management in 500 companies worldwide. Here he developed his "Absolutes of Quality Management."

After publishing *Quality Is Free* in 1979, he founded Philip Crosby Associates, Inc., and taught thousands of executives and managers through PCA's "Quality College." In 1985, PCA was the first U.S. consulting firm to go public. He retired in 1991, but continues to write, conduct seminars, and give lectures.

His books include: *Cutting the Cost of Quality* (1966, 1987); *The Art of Getting Your Own Sweet Way* (1972, 1981); *Quality Is Free* (1979); *Quality Without Tears* (1984); *Running Things* (1986); *The Eternally Successful Organization* (1988); *Let's Talk Quality* (1989); *Leading: The Art of Becoming an Executive* (1990); *Completeness* (1993); *Quality Is Still Free* (1995); and *The Absolutes of Leadership* (1996).

Phil Crosby is recognized throughout the world as the man who showed the U.S. how to define and implement quality. Mr. Crosby and his wife now live in Altamonte Springs, Florida, and Highlands, North Carolina.